Advances in Theoretical and Philosophical Psychology
Series Editor
Brent D. Slife
Brigham Young University

Situating Qualitative Methods in Psychological Science
Brian Schiff

Hermeneutic Moral Realism in Psychology: Theory and Practice
Brent D. Slife and Stephen Yanchar

A Humanities Approach to the Psychology of Personhood
Jeff Sugarman and Jack Martin

Subjectivity in Psychology in the Era of Social Justice
Bethany Morris, Chase O'Gwin, Sebastienne Grant, and Sakenya McDonald

For more information about this series, please visit: www.routledge.com/psychology/series/TPP

Subjectivity in Psychology in the Era of Social Justice

Bethany Morris, Chase O'Gwin,
Sebastienne Grant,
and Sakenya McDonald

R Routledge
Taylor & Francis Group

NEW YORK AND LONDON

First published 2020
by Routledge
52 Vanderbilt Avenue, New York, NY 10017

and by Routledge
2 Park Square, Milton Park, Abingdon, Oxon, OX14 4RN

Routledge is an imprint of the Taylor & Francis Group, an informa business

Library of Congress Cataloging-in-Publication Data
A catalog record for this book has been requested

ISBN: 978-0-367-42754-2 (hbk)
ISBN: 978-0-367-85488-1 (ebk)

Typeset in Times New Roman
by Apex CoVantage, LLC

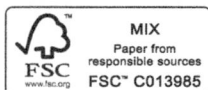

MIX
Paper from
responsible sources
FSC
www.fsc.org   FSC™ C013985

Printed in the United Kingdom
by Henry Ling Limited

To the psychology department at the University of West Georgia for their commitment to pushing the boundaries of psychology and Division 24 of the American Psychological Association for fostering such collaborations.

Contents

Acknowledgments

We would like to extend our thanks to Dr. Brent Slife for the opportunity to contribute to the Advances in Theoretical and Philosophical Psychology series.

We would also like to thank the faculty in the psychology department at the University of West Georgia for continuing to push the boundaries of psychology.

Bethany would like to thank her co-authors for sharing their creativity, brilliance, and kindness with her. She would also like to thank Dr. Fiona Ann Papps and Dr. Michael Arfken for showing her what psychology can be and should be. Finally, thanks to Alexander for the never-ending inspiration and support.

Sebastienne thanks her incredible co-authors and her amazing colleagues and students at Prescott College for providing limitless inspiration and hope.

Chase would first like to thank his ever-patient wife for all the extra work she has to put in so that he could get this written. Also he would like to personally thank his friends and teachers Brent Slife and Ed Gantt, his first guides on the path of theoretical and philosophical psychology, who taught him to look for the hidden assumptions and to turn old ideas upside-down and see what shakes out.

Sakenya recognizes her friend and mentor, Dr. Nancy Paxton, for her unwavering support, knowledge, and passion for the advancement of women scholars in all academic disciplines. She would also like to acknowledge her co-authors for modeling inclusivity through interdisciplinary collaboration. She would like to thank Prescott College for its tireless dedication to nurturing the academic integrity, creativity, and potential of all students. Lastly, she must acknowledge the bright and bold women of color scholars who have skillfully navigated the waters of academia; she is honored and forever grateful.

1   Introduction

The Era of Social Justice

It is our contention that we are in an era of social justice. By this we mean that social justice concerns, praxis, and ideology permeate much of the Western political and cultural discourse. This is not to say that social justice is a new phenomenon, as theorists and philosophers have been interrogating questions about what it means to be a just citizen in a just society since at least the ancient Greeks. However, the urgency around social justice issues, as well as some of the taken for granted assumptions about what constitutes social justice, seems to constitute much of the contemporary discourse. On the eve of another US presidential election, candidates are being asked to account for their views on diversity and inclusion, access to social services, and policies that have been identified as discriminatory or exclusive. It has also become standard to receive some sort of diversity and inclusion training at one's place of work, not to mention that many job applications within academia require the applicant to explain how one accommodates issues of diversity and inclusion in the classroom. Universities are beginning to offer classes and degrees in social justice, and positions in a variety of contexts are opening to accommodate those specialties. Furthermore, the locus of much of the discourse around social justice seems to be taking place on the internet in forums, blogs, and social media via tweets, posts, memes, and emojis. This not only means that issues and ideas reach more people faster than ever, but that debates and tensions also increase more rapidly around said issues, sometimes before proper fact checking can be done.

Contemporary social justice movements claim that social justice means the removal of barriers for social mobility, social support, and an equitable distribution of wealth (Kitching, 2001). While the concern seems to still be focused on economic equality and access to social services, people advocating for social justice have also included concerns such as representation in media, access to abortion and other reproductive health issues, being referred to by one's correct pronoun and gender identity in general, the disproportionate representation of minorities in the criminal justice system, and diversity within the workplace, to name only a very few. It would appear that social justice has become common parlance, and as a result the question about what it means to be socially just is a question psychologists must both investigate and interrogate. This book is an attempt to enter such discourse, with considerations about psychology's contributions to notions of social justice, and to consider the practicality of social justice given certain factors of modern subjectivity.

What Is Social Justice?

Social justice has undergone a number of conceptual transitions and instantiations. Roemer (1996) suggests that the problem of the allocation of resources in an equitable manner has been a concern for at least two millennia, citing both Aristotle and Plato as well as the Talmud as taking up the concern. Ornstein (2017) identifies the notion of social justice as originating in Christian doctrine, predicated on the command to help the less fortunate. Miller (2001) claims that though such concerns were evident earlier, the concept of social justice as we recognize it today was not introduced into political thought until the late 19th century in reaction to growing economic disparity and the role of the state. In claiming this, he also provides a framework from which to consider social justice concerns and initiatives, especially within the field of psychology. He delineates three factors that must be identified in considering social justice. The first is that the social sphere in question must be bounded, with group membership determinant so that members of the community can readily identify themselves as belonging to the same group, which Miller argues is most aptly recognized in the nation state. Second, Miller suggested that there needs to be an institutional body which can identify and regulate ideals of justice. Miller (2003) suggests that such a task may fall to the social sciences, "which enable the impact of institutional changes on individuals' life chances to be traced with a new-found precision and rigour" (as cited in Jackson, 2005, p. 357), an insight we will attempt to problematize with this book. Finally, it is assumed that the state has the agency to address and ameliorate inequitable conditions.

Ornstein (2017) claims that issues of social justice within the social sciences begins in the 1960s, with scientists and scholars attempting to consider issues of class and caste. This of course coincided with the various civil rights movements at the time, and soon social justice became associated with issues pertaining to race, class, gender, sexual orientation, and physical and mental health. The problem with a notion of justice premised on group membership of course is that social justice concerns can be claimed by any members of a group who believe they are oppressed or relegated to the margins of society. Social psychology tells us that members belonging to a group with a high degree of entitativity tends to share not only a social identity but also a worldview (Hogg, Hohman, & Rivera, 2008). This is why the National Socialist Party of Germany and the National Fascist Party of Italy were able to claim that their socioeconomic and nationalist propositions were in the interest of social justice and unity among the people. Social justice, then, cannot be understood as a colloquialism but rather a signifier that holds a number of potential interpretations and agendas for praxis.

Psychology and Social Justice: Conjunctions and Contradictions

As psychologists, we are intimately concerned with the ways in which issues of oppression and inequality affect one another, while also being aware of the fundamental issues that arise in attempting to have concrete operational definitions. As Louis, Mavor, Macchia, and Amiot (2014) explain, psychology is not a discipline constituted by a unified understanding of its parameters and praxes, nor does social justice have a consensus on its meaning, either within psychology or outside of the discipline. They go on to demonstrate that psychologists, because of our group alliances, are susceptible to the changing tides of our distinct disciplines, and therefore our perspectives on social justice, and more broadly ethics, may also fluctuate.

In order to navigate this uncertain terrain, we propose that as psychologists, we need to return to the taken for granted assumptions about subjectivity, both within our discipline as well as the disparate fields within psychology. The concept of subjectivity is one which is implicit in psychological discourses but not always explicitly articulated. In considering the ways in which subjectivity is constructed, understood, and implicated, perhaps we can also then think through the ways in which social justice is construed in relation to those assumptions about subjectivity.

Subjectivity and Psychology

In attempting to return to notions of subjectivity, we are of course reminded that this term also has had both a long and contentious history in philosophy, particularly continental philosophy, and can be traced to the work of

Descartes, Kant, and Hegel. For our purposes, we understand subjectivity as revolving around questions about the constitution of the individual and objectivity. To quote Hegel (1998), subjectivity can be understood as follows:

> The living substance, further, is that being which is truly subject, or, what is the same thing, is truly realized and actual (wirklich) solely in the process of positing itself, or in mediating with its own self its transitions from one state or position to the opposite. As subject it is pure and simple negativity, and just on that account a process of splitting up what is simple and undifferentiated, a process of duplicating and setting factors in opposition, which [process] in turn is the negation of this indifferent diversity and of the opposition of factors it entails. True reality is merely this process of reinstating self-identity, of reflecting into its own self in and from its other, and is not an original and primal unity as such, not an immediate unity as such. It is the process of its own becoming, the circle which presupposes its end as its purpose, and has its end for its beginning; it becomes concrete and actual only by being carried out, and by the end it involves.
>
> (para. 18)

For Hegel, a subject arises out of the structure of its own negation, its own alienation. In his own way, Freud took up this idea of subject-as-structure and would popularize the idea of the unconscious and a subject to whom parts of itself were alien and inaccessible (Freud, 2005). One notes the structuring point was speaking, as opposed to Gestalt (e.g., as elaborated by Merleau-Ponty (1967, 2002), leaving the unsayable, the unsaid, as its residues—hence the unconscious. However, the subject would interact with the world though the use of a specialized sub-function of the subject Freud dubbed Ich, often translated as Ego. This term would be picked up by popular psychology as a way to describe one's sense of subjectivity and even by cognitive psychology as the seat of cognition (Carhart-Harris & Friston, 2010).

The purpose of this book is to think through the ways in which subjectivity can be said to be constituted, affected, and penetrated by social discourses, with concerns for being socially just. It is the authors' intention to consider subjectivity as a locus of these discourses through which to consider the implicit intersection of the individual and the social, where each constitutes the other. In order to do this, each chapter is helmed by an individual author, lending his or her expertise to questions pertaining to subjectivity and social justice.

In Chapter 2, Sakenya McDonald demonstrates the ways in which critical psychology can come to inform psychology about the role of subjectivity in social justice issues. She focuses specifically on the role psychology and education have had on the creation of apathetic subjectivities through hyper-competitiveness and emphasis on personal worth determined by capital. This chapter grounds our concerns as localized within neoliberal capitalism, asking how it implicitly produces problematic subjectivities. This allows Sebastienne Grant to further discuss in Chapter 3 the ways in which psychology has contributed to the construction of subjectivities that are resistant to or hinder social justice. She takes up the argument that the field of psychology unintentionally contributes to constructions of modern Western subjectivities that are largely incompatible with the ideals, values, and goals of social justice. She argues that psychology could promote social justice by mindfully contributing to the construction of more socially just subjectivities. This follows the work of psychologists such as Philip Cushman and David Loy, who have claimed that modern subjectivities are marked by a deep sense of emptiness, resulting in personally and socially harmful traits and behaviors (such as individualism, materialism, narcissism, territorialism, and greed) aimed at covering over or filling up their lacking interiors. She contends that with intention and effort, however, psychologists can address the issue of the empty self *and* promote socially just subjectivities.

In Chapter 4, Bethany Morris considers the responses to social justice concerns at the industrial and organizational level, looking specifically at diversity and inclusion initiatives. She argues that such initiatives are ultimately conceived of through a combination of cognitive psychology discourses and neoliberal capitalist demands and are thus problematic for those interested in social justice concerns. She uses a Lacanian psychoanalytic perspective to explore the construction and relationship to the Other that is reified in both cognitive psychology and diversity initiatives. A Lacanian perspective also allows us to consider how we might confront, consider, and be compassionate in the face of alterity in ways that does not demand assimilation into an exploitative capitalist system.

In Chapter 5, Chase O'Gwin explores some of the problematic manifestations of social justice in popular culture as a way to explore social justice ideology and the symptoms that have arisen from it. This chapter will focus on two of the most prominent symptoms. The first goes by many names: the Tumblr Social Justice Warrior, the Facebook Activist, the call-out troll, and so forth, wherein social justice causes are seen as an opportunity for social performance rather than a chance for participating in actual activism. The second is the nature and status of being "woke." He investigates how these present symptoms have arisen, particularly in an age where Baudrillard's predictions of a reality as simulacrum have already come to pass or have come perilously close to doing so. Furthermore, he advances the implications this has on the current social justice movement, exploring the problematic nature of symptoms as part of a social/cultural ideological injunction of "justice for all" that is impossible to meet. Finally, through the theories of Emmanuel Levinas, he considers some possible solutions to this predicament in social justice initiatives in contemporary Western society.

References

Carhart-Harris, R. L., & Friston, K. J. (2010). The default-mode, ego-functions and free-energy: A neurobiological account of Freudian ideas. *Brain, 133*(4), 1265–1283.

Freud, S. (2005). *The unconscious.* London: Penguin Books.

Hegel, G.W.F. (1998). *Phenomenology of spirit.* New Delhi: Motilal Banarsidass.

Hogg, M. A., Hohman, Z. P., & Rivera, J. E. (2008). Why do people join groups? Three motivational accounts from social psychology. *Social and Personality Compass, 2*(3), 1269–1280.

Jackson, B. (2005). The conceptual history of social justice. *Political Studies Review, 3,* 356–373.

Kitching, G. M. (2001). *Seeking social justice through globalization: Escaping a nationalist perspective.* University Park, PA: Penn State University.

Louis, W. R., Mavor, K. I., La Macchia, S. T., & Amiot, C. E. (2014). Social justice and psychology: What it is, and what should be. *Journal of Theoretical and Philosophical Psychology, 34*(1), 14–27.

Merleau-Ponty, M. (1967). *The Structure of Behavior.* London: Beacon Press.

Merleau-Ponty, M. (2002). *Phenomenology of Perception.* London: Routledge.

Miller, D. (2001). *Principles of social justice.* Cambridge, MA: Harvard University Press.

Miller, D. (2003). A response. In D. A. Bell & A. De-Shalit's (Eds.), *Forms of justice: A critical perspective on David Miller's political philosophy* (pp. 349–372). Oxford: Rowman & Littlefield.

Ornstein, A. C. (2017). Social justice: History, purpose, and meaning. *Social Science and Public Policy, 54,* 541–548.

Roemer, J. E. (1996). *Theories of distributive justice.* Cambridge, MA: Harvard University Press.

2 Systemic Apathy, Subjectivity, and Social Justice in Psychology and Education

The rationale informing the use of critical psychology as an analytical lens through which the relationship between social justice and psychology is articulated is relatively straightforward. Critical psychology encourages an evocative counter-narrative to the prevailing commentary on the form and function of mainstream psychology. Factions, such as psycho-politics and psychological imperialism, were constructed by ideologies rooted in oppressive, neoliberal logic that contribute to social decay (Hook et al., 2004; Teo, 2015). Disruptive factions create barriers to progress, and critical psychology posits that unless these barriers are actively scrutinized, the discipline of psychology will continue to perpetuate upon society practices that are exclusionary and prohibitive. For example, practices that fail to acknowledge power differentials in doctor–patient relationships or ignore the cultural significance of community-focused healing in certain groups are, according to critical psychologists, reinforcing a neoliberal agenda that is antithetical to the premise of social justice.

According to Portelli and Konecny (2013), neoliberal culture "dominates the 'Western' world" and "militates against the growth of any robust democratic culture" (p. 91). Areas such as social, community, and critical psychology object to the neoliberal institutionalization of the discipline of psychology because, in the words of Henry Giroux (2006):

> Neoliberal ideology, with its merciless emphasis on deregulation and privatization, has found its material expression in an all-out attack on democratic values and social relations . . . public services such as health care, childcare, public assistance, education, and transportation are now subject to the rules of the market. Forsaking the public good for the private good and representing the needs of the corporate and private sector as the only source of sound investment.
>
> (p. 24)

Noted experts in various fields of psychology acknowledge the risks associated with focusing solely on the therapies that isolate the individual from the community in efforts to assuage conditions that are deemed to be undesirable (Fox, Prilleltensky, & Austin, 2009; Teo, 2015; Hook et al., 2004). When neoliberalism dictates how a society distributes social resources such as health care and education, two institutions influenced by psychological theory and practice, it is often the most impoverished communities and individuals that are the most impacted. It can be argued that neoliberalism isolates individual responses that are systematically perceived as being in defiance of what has been established as being objective, normalized, and consensual. In this chapter, we will examine ways in which a neoliberal-centric regulation of the subject permeates the institution of education, how the discipline of psychology facilitates regulation, mitigation and remedy, and lastly, how the theme of social justice serves as an impetus to anticipated reform.

Social Justice and the Subject

Defining social justice is an elusive process, as Novak (2009) noted: "whole books and treatises have been written about social justice without ever offering a definition of it. It is allowed to float in the air as if everyone will recognize an instance of it when it arises" (p. 1). Scholarship on the subject is indeterminate as to whether social justice is exclusive to basic liberties, fair distribution of goods, the elimination of oppression, or equal and equitable participation in social and political life (Thrift & Sugarman, 2019). Most scholars agree that, conceptually, social justice is defined by its proximity to injustice or to what extent institutional factors exacerbate the injustice gap. The injustice gap is important because, according to Alim, Due, and Strelan (2019), the injustice gap is "a discrepancy between expected (fair) treatment and actual (unfair) treatment" (p. 255). It is up to the subject to determine the severity of the gap and what course of action is most likely to mitigate damages; however, in instances of systemic injustice, individuals "rarely, if ever, have recourse to such [mitigating] processes" (p. 256). Systemic injustices, or "situations where individuals have experienced injustice due to the machinations of a particular system under which they have been living" (Alim et al., 2019, p. 256), are embedded in neoliberal best practices. Therefore, it is reasonable to conclude that institutions operating with neoliberal principles are limited in proximity to social justice best practices, and furthermore, individuals subjugated by these institutions rarely experience equitable, fair, and just treatment.

Critical psychologists and other experts unequivocally recognize the significance of power dynamics within institutionalized settings and how unacknowledged power acts as a repellent to actions that are deemed to be in the interests of the greater good (minority). To illustrate, Blader and Chen (2012) found, in a study on status, power, and justice, consistent evidence indicating "high power was associated with relatively less fairness" (p. 16) and Sharma (2009) wrote, "power without justice is tyranny" (p. 1). Power leads to injustice when it neglects, obfuscates, and marginalizes multitudinous voices, especially when those voices represent a majority presence. Noted scholar and expert on postcolonialism, Trinh Minh-ha (1989), explained as follows:

> One can date it back to the immemorial days when a group of mighty men (minority placement) attributed to itself a central, dominating position vis-à-vis other groups; overvalued its particularities and achievements, adopted a projective attitude toward those it classified among the out-group (majority placement); and wrapped itself up in its own thinking, interpreting the out-group through the in-group mode of reasoning while claiming to speak the minds of both the in-group and the out-group.
>
> (p. 1)

Shifting the focus to neoliberalism, it becomes evident that contemporary society is in a state of social decay due to the greed, corruption, and apathy of colonization that currently manifests in neoliberalism. Groups in positions of power constitute such a small percentage of the population and are thereby incapable of appropriately considering the needs of the majority. This imbalance, according to Kukathas (1998), favors the voice of the minority, which causes a cacophony of voices of which only the loudest, and often most disruptive, is heard. In summary, unchecked institutional power serves the demands of the few and, by default, incentivizes systemic attitudes and values that encourage apathy over empathy. For example, in 2012, the US Census Bureau issued a news press release titled "U.S. Census Bureau Projections Show a Slower Growing, Older, More Diverse Nation a Half Century from Now," in which projections indicated that by 2060 minorities, defined as "all but the single-race, non-Hispanic white population" will constitute 57 percent of the nation's population. That indicates that the current cultural climate is rapidly shifting and that those in the most established positions of power will constitute less than 43 percent of the US population, therefore constituting a *minority* group (US Census Bureau).

This data is significant because it demonstrates that despite impending fluctuations in what is projected to represent the majority group in the United States current majority groups aggressively seek "to speak the minds of both the in-group and the out-group." Critical psychologists warn that this behavior is consistent with the rigidity in power and at the core of social injustice. When institutions, such as education, are constructed on neoliberal power hierarchies, the institutions' original function is altered, and subjects who fail to assimilate to existing power dynamics are left exposed and vulnerable.

To clarify, an institution is defined as "a significant practice, relationship, or organization in a society or culture" (psychology). As such, the discipline of psychology is a powerful institution onto itself; the implementation of psychological theory or practice is embedded into every major aspect of modern culture. According to Hook et al. (2004), "psychology is always—even in its most everyday and mundane forms—*profoundly political, profoundly involved in the reproduction and extension of relations of power and control*" (p. 13). Therefore, to posit social justice within institutionalized psychology, one must begin by spotlighting the neoliberal agenda and the ways in which it informs the subjective experience, specifically attitudes, values, and realities. From there, it becomes possible to isolate systemic inequities and inconsistencies while intentionally focusing on narrowing the injustice gap.

Subjectivity, Institutional Oppression, and Differing Realities

The exercise of minimizing the relationship between social injustice and subjectivity is problematic to the development of more inclusive psychological fields, but many psychologists, especially in critical, social, and community-based areas, are working to ameliorate these problems. Sugarman (2015) acknowledged that "as long as we are focused on ourselves, our desires, ends, and pursuits are detached from the collective concerns, and the sociopolitical status quo goes largely unexamined and unquestioned" (p. 113). For psychology to remain relevant, it must exemplify subjectivity; in other words, psychology must continue to be shaped by experiences and culture while simultaneously retaining a sense of true purpose and position in the natural world. In fact, according to Montero (1982), the ideal subject is described as "active" and not merely an "inert receptor of external action" (p. 17). Action manifests through the individual as "consciousness and agency" and drives the construction of the subject; "for this reason, the subject is seen as the seat of awareness, will, liberty, reason, and morality"

(Cronick, 2002, p. 531). Therefore, it is reasonable to conclude that subjectivity informs interpretation and perception and validates experiences and realities.

Consider examples of subjective qualia such as describing the feelings a person experiences when viewing the color blue, listening to a symphony, or performing a rigorous physical activity. Social science describes subjectivity as an effect of relations of power while cultural studies believe subjectivity is culturally constructed and neither is incorrect. Sheikh (2017) suggests that one becomes a subject via cultural immersion and, as such, subjectivity "reflects the social processes that constitute us as subjects" (p. 2). Concerning subjectivities, Kelly (2013) noted, "the subject is understood as something that must be constructed" (p. 513) and "what we take ourselves to be, then affects who we are" (p. 515). Foucault postulated that subjectivities are not universal, but cultural, and therefore subjectivity is formed by the culture a person is born into or the proximity of a persons' position (positionality) to a place of power or privilege. As such, subjectivity aids in the construction of reality, and while the philosophy of psychology accounts for this phenomenon, neoliberal attitudes embedded in psychological theory and practice makes little concession for individuals whose reality differs from those empowered by neoliberalism. Not only does this create opportunities for furthering the injustice gap, it spills over into other institutions, such as education, that are influenced by psychology, thereby multiplying the oppressive effects to the detriment of those dependent on an equitable distribution of resources.

For example, consider what happens when a psychologist fails to manage multicultural due diligence, ignoring how culture informs subjectivity, and places an individual on a course of action that further alienates or isolates. Deutsch (2006, as cited in Cameron Kelly & Varghese, 2018) would define this behavior as indicative of institutional oppression or "the mistreatment [intentional or not] of people of a particular group that is enforced by society and its institutions" (p. 875). Institutional oppression contributes to the subjugation of the subject, which in turn creates a more distinct awareness of how far removed an individual is from the dominating culture. The discipline of psychology has evolved under Westernized culture, and contemporary psychology still embodies many of the values and beliefs of a society that is hyper-focused on uniformity and the establishment of one "viable" way of conducting business. Subjectivity that is created beyond the scope of Westernized thought has long been believed to be defective, and psychology is complicit in alienating entire groups of persons. In the education setting, these groups include, but are not limited to, students of color, students with disabilities, students who are economically disadvantaged and students who are non-gender conforming.

Within the institute of education, students who fail to construct a subjectivity that focuses on individual and competitive pursuits (Fox et al., 2009, p. 6) or embody neoliberal, capitalist ideologies (Sugarman, 2015) often experience alienation. Marx's alienation theory proposes, in brief, that an individual might suffer from a lack of personal identity with the product of their labor and struggle with feelings of domination and exploitation (Marx, 1978). Often, marginalized students possess a reality where products of labor, such as standardized testing, are not designed for their success but rather are created by individuals whose implicit biases dominate and exploit perceived cultural differences. Also embedded in this alienation process are any accompanying psychological challenges faced by students who are already isolated. To receive a diagnosis of ADHD, depression, or personality disorder without considering relevant cultural context or existent power dynamics places them further from positions of power, leaving them vulnerable to the persuasion of the individuals society has conditioned them to trust.

In *Sane Society*, Fromm (1956/2008) elucidated the role that culture and society play in the formation of subjectivity. The apparent dysfunction in the mental health of oppressed people, when defined by those who constitute the domineering social character, is often a subjectivity striving to express itself in its purest form despite opposition. Fromm explained:

> The basic psychic needs stemming from the peculiarities of human existence must be satisfied in one form or other, unless man is to become insane . . . if one of the basic necessities . . . has found no fulfillment, insanity is the result; if it is satisfied but in an unsatisfactory way—considering the nature of human existence—neurosis (either manifest or in the form of a socially patterned defect) is the consequence. Man has to relate himself to others; but if he does it in a symbiotic or alienated way, he loses his independence and integrity; he is weak, suffers, becomes hostile, or apathetic; only if he can relate himself to others in a loving way does he feel one with them and at the same time preserve his integrity.
>
> (p. 66)

Fromm's theory on the function of social character suggests that social character exists to encourage members of a society to behave in ways that are not the result of conscious decision (Fromm, 1956/2008; Brookfield, 2002). In other words, social character expects "the members of the society . . . to behave in such a way as to be able to function in the sense required by the social system" (Fromm, 1956/2008, p. 77). Additionally, Fromm (1956/2008) argued that the social character is the core of a structure shared by most members of a culture (pp. 76–77). Too often, the science of psychology, or the universality of it, fails to account for the many ways in which concepts "are socially and historically constituted and value-laden" (Teo, 2015). Fox et al. (2009) observed, "psychologist too often forget that many of the behaviours they and others around them engage in everyday reflect culture and history rather than universal inevitability" (pp. 5–6). Individuals constructing subjectivities based on cultural interpretations of experiences that deviate from the Westernized standard are encouraged to assimilate into social systems that are neglectful of their needs. Far too often, however, the assimilation process retards the growth and development of marginalized groups.

Therefore, it is logical to deduce that a student whose social character is shaped by a culture beyond the realm of neoliberalism may present with a mental health status that is "characterized by a sense of identity based on one's experience of self as the subject and agent of one's powers, by the grasp of reality inside and outside of ourselves" (Fromm, 1956/2018, p. 67). This concept of *differing realities* is not foreign to scholars in fields that are often intensely focused on issues related to social justice. Patricia Hill Collins (1995), a black feminist theorist who has written extensively about differing realities, explained that "black women's political and economic status provides them with a distinctive set of experiences that offers a different view of material reality than that available to any other groups" (p. 339). Referencing her personal experiences as a female scholar of color, Hill Collins asserted that academic communities are ill-equipped to ask "the kind of questions" that would satisfy the unique needs of black women scholars because the dominating worldview "reflects a basic lack of familiarity with black women's reality" (p. 342).

To illustrate, contemporary educational models suggest implementing diversity and equity programs and initiatives as a means for recognizing how differing realities inform one's educational experience. While studies indicate that most of these programs have some success, critical discourse analysis indicates that these programs are equally as divisive and often reinforce neoliberal ideologies through language (Iverson, 2007). In a subsequent chapter, we will discuss further how attempts to promote diversity and inclusion in the university setting often end up propagating and bolstering neoliberal capitalist agendas. Additionally, psychology is often intimately involved in the construction of the policies and procedures that guide the formation of campus diversity and equity initiatives. An error in psychology, according to Fox et al. (2009) is that "mainstream psychology's Westernized individualistic worldview . . . blinds people to the impact of their actions and lifestyles on others who remain oppressed" (p. 6). This demonstrates a need for greater accountability in the discipline of psychology and a critical analysis of the rampant systemic apathy that has manifest in the institutions serviced by psychological inquiry, theory, and practice.

Systemic Apathy in Psychology and Education

Subjectivity is a process of becoming; it is the simultaneous occupation of two states of being: governing and being governed. Foucault believed that the word "subject" was dualistic in nature, with both aspects being suggestive of a form of power which subjugates and makes subject to (Ball & Olmedo, 2013). Several areas of psychology posit that subjectivity is fluid and dynamic because society and culture share the same traits and are direct contributors to how subjectivity is constructed. Yet, Gump (2010) wrote in her article "Reality Matters: The Shadow of Trauma on African American Subjectivity" that few psychoanalytic theories "accord culture a role" when discussing subjectivity, especially when considering subjectivity in individuals belonging to non-dominant groups. Gump (2010) asserted that "this silence distorts and constricts our understanding of all subjects, but is particularly pernicious for the non-dominant, it renders significant aspects of their subjectivities invisible" (p. 42). As a result, individuals in non-dominant groups are never offered the proverbial seat at the table, which suppresses the acquisition of knowledge required for the discipline of psychology to remain relevant and inclusive. Ball and Olmedo (2013) summarized, "the constraining historical, political, and economic contextual factors are therefore central to the understanding . . . of possibilities and practices through which the subject actively constitutes him/herself" (p. 87). So what is silencing these conversations?

Critical analysis indicates that there is no definitive answer to the question of why there is still some resistance to re-examining existing power structures in the field of psychology. Examining institutional power differentials explains how one group is able to dominate another group, as demonstrated through Trinh Minh-ha's representation of in- and out-groups. Neoliberal ideology provides context to another possibility, one that suggests that individuals are willing to conform to a dominant social character to compete, to advance their position, or to avoid negative perceptions, as noted by Ball and Olmedo (2013):

Neoliberalism requires and enacts a "new type of individual" . . . formed within the logic of competition. The apparatuses of neoliberalism are seductive, enthralling and overbearingly necessary. It is a "new" moral system that subverts and re-orients us to its truths and ends. It makes us responsible for our performance and for the performance of others. We are burdened with the responsibility to perform, and if we do not we are in danger of being seen as irresponsible.

(p. 89)

Another answer, and the one that is argued in this chapter, is found in understanding how attitudes and emotions, specifically apathy, influence action.

Apathy is defined as a lack of motivation (Marin, 1991) or a lack of interest or emotion (Van Reekum, Stuss, & Ostrander, 2005). Subtypes of apathy include cognitive, emotional-affective, and auto-activation, and apathy can be "both a symptom and a syndrome" (Radakovic & Abrahams, 2014). Apathy is both cause and effect; it can manifest as a symptom of some deeper mental or physical condition or it can be a by-product of one's perceptions or interpretations. For example, activists who are unable to connect to the economic or political resources needed to inspire social reform often experience burnout or become apathetic to their cause. When this occurs within a system, such as the education system, it may be referred to as *systemic apathy*. Systemic apathy is a way of viewing complex problems and expanding the discourse on indifference and inaction as forms of social injustice. To illustrate, consider the history of apathetic attitudes toward non-dominant groups in education and how these attitudes contributed to institutional racism, the advancement of neoliberalism, and traumatized subjectivities.

In 1904, French psychologist Alfred Binet produced the Binet Scale of intelligence, or the first test designed to measure mild developmental disabilities in children. This test, according to Gould (1996), was intended to be used on small children, and Binet made no claims suggesting test scores were related to hereditary or innate intelligence. However, according to Au (2013), in the 20th century US cognitive psychologists Yerkers, Goddard, and Terman, supported by educational philanthropists including Andrew Carnegie, embarked on a campaign endorsing the use of Binet's test as a means of advancing race and class politics. The rigor present in the studies conducted can be considered dubious at best as observed by Karier (1972): "Terman developed questions . . . he believed were necessary for achievement in ascending the hierarchical occupational structure" (p. 163, as cited in Au, 2013, p. 8). Individuals belonging to targeted groups, namely blacks and non-Europeans, criticized IQ tests as being biased yet under a neoliberal agenda, IQ tests in educational settings became the gold standard for measuring and predicting intelligence.

By 1932, the majority of large city schools in the United States were operating with IQ and standardized testing as primary resources for sorting students into ability groups or determining admission status (Au, 2013). The discipline of psychology and psychologists such as Yerkers, Goddard, and Terman propagated the belief that certain ethnic groups were predisposed to a higher measure of intelligence, as noted by Karier (1972):

> It was men like Thorndike, Terman and Goddard, supported by corporate wealth, who successfully persuaded teacher, administrators and lay school boards to classify and standardize the school's curriculum with a differentiated track system based on ability and values of the corporate liberal society.
>
> (p. 166)

Fast-forwarding to the current era reveals systems in play that are still hyper-focused on endorsing classist, racist, and sexist structures. Lakes and Carter (2011) observed that "the ultimate goal of neoliberal reformers is to convert educational systems into markets, as much as possible privatize educational services" (p. 108), and that some propose the development is already in process in the form of "publicly-supported vouchers for private school tuition, high-stakes standardized testing . . . scripted curricula, and, in general, the underfunding of public education" (p. 108). When the dominant social character of a society views education as a market, where students, teachers, and administrators are viewed as capital, an apathetic attitude is formed. The greater emphasis is placed on performance and profit rather than equity and fairness, which in turn increases the injustice gap for those who are perceived as underperforming or unprofitable.

In summary, systemic apathy in education and psychology is rooted in power. The in-group determines the needs of the out-group with no regard to the historical, political, economic, or cultural factors that shape the social character and subjectivities of the out-group. The dominant majority lacks diversity and inclusivity and therefore is disconnected from the desires and needs of others. Subjectivity is colonized through inappropriate action (overgeneralizations about the best way to distribute resources to "the other") and inaction (failure to change policy and procedure that actually results in progress). As if this is not damaging enough, systemic apathy is insidious and eventually will manifest in both the subjugator and subjugated. In the educational setting, this results in psychological positive feedback loop as demonstrated by analyzing the results of the Latane and Darley experiments also known as Bystander Apathy.

Bystanders, Social Disruptors, and the Subject

As an analogy to demonstrate the impacts of systemic apathy in institution-alized education, the Bystander Apathy experiments contextualize social function in situations where mitigation is needed but not offered. The crisis of the relationship between psychology and education concerns those moti-vated by social justice and requires intervention based on three of the five characteristics of an emergency as proposed in Latane and Darley's work. These characteristics include any situation that "involves threat or harm, is unusual, and requires instant action" (pp. 245–246). According to Latane and Darley (1969) the intervention process involves five steps:

1. Bystanders must *notice* that something is happening,
2. One must *interpret* the event; the decision must be made that some-thing is wrong,
3. One must decide they have a *responsibility to act*,
4. Deciding on what *form of assistance* can be offered,
5. After the decision is made, it must then be *implemented*.

(pp. 247–248)

Latane and Darley argued that this model may be "too rational," citing several reasons including how an individual's perception of "reality" (sub-jectivity) or "potential consequences for self" may result in vacillation on behalf of the bystander (pp. 247–248).

Latane and Darley also recognizes how the introduction of different vari-ables to the model may require modifications to the intervention plan. The current educational model is flawed (Kozol, 1992), and parents, students, teachers, administrators, and policy makers are all capable of initiating change but at variable levels of power. The specifics of how this power is unfairly distributed, and how this inequity can greatly hinder change, is better explained by examining Latane and Darley's Experiment Number 2, "A Lady in Distress" (1969). In this experiment, male undergraduate stu-dents at Columbia University were invited to participate in a survey with compensation promised at $2 per person. Upon arrival, a female organizer invited participants in and then went into partitioned space under the guise that she needed to retrieve items. While in the space, the female organizer (a member of Latane and Darley's research team) played a pre-recorded tape with crashing sounds and screams that replicated a situation of her falling from a tall stepladder ("The Emergency"). Latane and Darley used four dif-ferent conditions identified as "Alone" ($n = 26$), "Stooge" ($n = 14$), "Strang-ers" ($n = 20$ pairs), and "Friends" ($n = 20$ pairs). For the sake of this analogy, the "Alone" group represents individuals with critical consciousness, or a healthy subjectivity, in social context. The "Stooge" group represents one kind of social disruptor, *false consciousness*, or those unable to recognize oppression because of a blind acceptance of social classes (Fromm, 1976; Brookfield, 2002).

False consciousness manifests in three ways; the first is as a social disruptor known as *pluralistic ignorance*, or a state of willful apathy or lack of concern, based on an interpretation of how others, especially those in positions of power, respond to a situation (Latane & Darley, 1969). The second is individuals willingly perpetrating social injustice (Johnston-Goodstar & VeLure Roholt, 2017; Kozol, 1992) under the belief that those who fail to conform to the dominant social character are "bad apples" (Fox et al., 2009). Finally, false consciousness manifests in individuals whose subjectivity or reality differs from the established social character and are convinced that their problems are individual and not social. Examples of this in education include students who are convinced that their inability to achieve and excel in school is the result of a mental or emotional disorder (Johnston-Goodstar & VeLure Roholt, 2017; Kozol, 1992; Perry, Steele, & Hilliard, 2003). Each of these examples are symbolic petri dishes for the cultivation of systemic apathy or willful neglect of social responsibility, as Fox et al. (2009) wrote: "blaming individuals for their widely shared problems . . . makes people less likely to advocate for social change" (pp. 7–8).

To illustrate, referencing Latane and Darley's Experiment Number 2, 70 percent of participants in the "Alone" group responded and offered assistance. By contrast, in the "Stooge" group only 7 percent of participants offered help, which represents a difference in response rates that was "significant" ($p < .001$) (Latane & Darley, 1969, p. 255). So, what was the differing variable between these two groups? In the "Alone" group, participants were alone with the female organizer, whereas in the "Stooge" group, a stranger/stooge was present and had been given explicit instructions to "be as passive as possible." This was demonstrated in how the stooge responded during the emergency, "he looked up, shrugged his shoulders, and continued working on his questionnaire" (Latane & Darley, 1969, p. 255). For unexplained reasons, participants in the study seemed to model the apathetic attitude of the stooge although there was no pre-defined power dynamic between participant and stooge. What was most telling, however, was how the participants categorized their response to the situation at the end of the experiment. Latane and Darley (1969) observed that

> subjects in the passive confederate condition reported, on average, that they were "very little" influenced by the stooge, a claim which was

directly "counter to the experiment results, in which . . . subjects in the Stooge condition were most inhibited by the other's actions."

(p. 256)

What was also remarkable in Latane and Darley's (1969) observations of the "Stooge" condition participant responses was that during the experiment, subjects "seemed upset and confused during the emergency and frequently glanced at the passive confederate" (p. 255). In an educational sense, systemic apathy is generated in like manner through another social disruptor, *pluralistic ignorance*, or as Latane and Darley (1969) explained, situations where "until someone acts, each person sees only the other non-responding bystanders, and is likely to be influenced to act himself" (p. 248). Inclusive to pluralistic ignorance are feelings of anger, confusion, and hopelessness (Latane & Darley, 1969), which may be more pronounced when the non-responsive individuals exude power and authority. It is not unreasonable, therefore, to conclude that there is a state of emergency in the educational system and that indifference (as the result of power inequities) may inadvertently cause systemic apathy demonstrated in the form of pluralistic ignorance.

When members of a non-dominant group are subjected to systemic apathy in one of two forms, false consciousness or pluralistic ignorance, what results is a positive feedback loop, or in systems theory context, a process that occurs in a system that exasperates minor fluctuations. In educational institutions, systemic apathy creates a positive feedback loop because systemic apathy is bilateral and feeds itself. To illustrate, consider the system of "tracking" that exists in some educational settings. According to Johnston-Goodstar and VeLure Roholt (2017), Native American students are tracked based on their success in "Eurocentric curriculum and pedagogical styles" (p. 40). Teachers observe that several students are "gifted" and would thrive in conducive environments where their differing realities are acknowledged. However, when these same students fail to conform to a social character that excludes their cultural, historical, and social experiences and the subjectivities they construct, they are labeled as "naughty . . . then they get labeled as Special Ed" (Johnston-Goodstar & VeLure Roholt, 2017, p. 40). A vital question to ask is: who is responsible for the labeling of these students?

Historically, that responsibility has been bestowed upon trained practitioners within the discipline of psychology. However, as Gump and Hill Collins observed, there is often silence and limited accountability from the established social character which facilitates neoliberal beliefs, such as "failure to achieve is deemed one's own fault" (Lakes & Carter, 2011,

p. 108). Once a student has been victimized by either institutional racism or systemic apathy, they are often subjugated to labels that they actively reject:

> For one student who just "couldn't listen to that bullshit no more," the daily onslaught of microinsults led to outright anger, but it could lead to conformity or quiet disengagement that isn't necessarily "labeled" but results in negative outcomes like truancy or "dropout."
>
> (Johnston-Goodstar & VeLure Roholt, 2017, p. 40)

A positive feedback loop then develops as follows: systemic apathy from the dominant group becomes a catalyst for institutional racism, which fuels the victimization of students through tactics such as tracking, which inspires feelings of hopelessness and apathy in the non-dominant group. In other words, the prophecy becomes self-fulfilling. Due to apathetic attitudes towards "the other," the in-group fails to acknowledge the role that culture plays in the construction of subjectivity in minoritized students. Students contending with these misnomers (*under-performing, low-achieving, behavioral problems*) and stigmas develop apathetic feelings about their ability to exist as part of the social character. They are no longer able to realize success in the context of a reality that is not their own and are not offered the equitable distribution of resources needed to locate and utilize systemic leverage points.

Donella Meadow's (1997) system theory approach suggests that the term *leverage point* refers to the "place within a complex system where small shifts in one thing . . . can produce big changes in everything" (p. 1). Meadows (1997) suggested that the most dynamic leverage point is *transcending paradigms*, but its antecedent is *careful deliberation concerning the mindset or paradigm driving the system*. Identifying systemic apathy through careful scrutiny of institutionalized structures is what Latane and Darley (1969) would consider as the first step in the intervention process or noticing "that something is happening" and being "willing to remove oneself from private or distractive thought" (p. 247). *Interpreting* the events, the second step, would require critical analysis of systemic flaws and their effect on subjectivity and social justice by those who possess the power to disrupt the positive feedback loop. Action is only made possible when individuals, including students, teachers, administrators, and policy makers acknowledge their *responsibility to act* (Latane & Darley, 1969). Critical psychologists and other scholars from various fields of study including the humanities, anthropology, philosophy, and sociology are actively collaborating to quell the effects of systemic apathy. Researchers are seeking out new methodologies, such as transformative paradigms, and examining "advantaged groups prosocial emotions" (Thomas, McGarty, & Mavor, 2009) with the hopes that their discoveries will illuminate methods dismantling attitudes that are diametrically opposed to the very nature of education.

Recommendations for Remediation

According to Donna M. Mertens (2007), "the transformative paradigm provides a framework for examining assumptions that explicitly address power issues, social justice, and cultural complexity throughout the research process" (pp. 212–213). Realizing that power is embedded in everything political, including society, the transformative paradigm methodology presents methods by which researchers become skilled in recognizing and addressing power differentials and, therefore, able to seek out viable solutions to contemporary problems. Confronting ways in which realities are shaped by elements, including the social and cultural communities to which one belongs, the transformative paradigm challenges researchers to acknowledge the idea of *differing realities*, or subjectivities, when considering the four research assumptions.

The ontological assumption in transformative paradigm suggests that "there are multiple realities that are socially constructed" (Mertens, 2007, p. 216). To design obtainable results, researchers must account for the various cultural factors that construct subjectivity, and more importantly, "what are the social justice implications of accepting reality that has not been subjected to a critical analysis on the basis of power differentials" (Mertens, 2007, p. 216). This is vital because one of the leverage points that Meadows (1997) describes as being most efficient is deliberating on the mindset driving the current paradigm. By recognizing where power lies in a paradigm and how that power isolates, marginalizes, and obfuscates, it is possible to construct a new, transformative paradigm offering forms of assistance that are relevant and meaningful.

For example, Thomas et al. (2009) conducted research examining the role of prosocial emotions in transforming apathy into movement. When apathy is present and active in a system, privileged and dominating groups often see minimal incentive in initiating change, especially if neoliberalism determines that change is a threat to current market profitability. Freire (1970/2005) suggested that oppressors will even offer false generosity, or situations where "in order to have the continued opportunity to express their 'generosity,' the oppressors must perpetuate injustice as well" (p. 44). Rather than inspire true change the oppressor suffers from a form of Munchausen syndrome by proxy; they facilitate injustices, feign concern, and then seek to close the injustice gap in ways that are self-serving. In this case, the transformation is disingenuous and inauthentic, lacking the true prosocial emotions required to facilitate change.

Thomas et al. (2009) cited the words of Carl Jung (1938), "there can be no transforming of darkness into light and of apathy into movement without emotion" (p. 32, cited on p. 310). The emotions of those in advantaged groups differ from those in disadvantaged groups and Thomas et al. (2009) examined how advantage groups relate to the deprivation of others. What was discovered is that prosocial emotions such as "pride and hope may have much to offer people seeking to create inclusive, agentic movements defined by positive affect" (Thomas et al., 2009, p. 329). In other words, it is possible to implement systemic change, but in order to do so the emotions driving positive affect must suppress exasperating conditions such as false generosity, pluralistic ignorance, westernized individualism, and most of all, apathy.

In *Pedagogy of the Oppressed*, Freire (1970/2005) wrote, "This, then, is the great humanistic and historical task of the oppressed: to liberate themselves and their oppressors as well" (p. 44). Liberation is not an easy task because it must take place on multiple levels; the mind must be liberated, the spirit must be liberated, and the body must also be liberated. The totality of the being must be free to develop identity and character that is defined by their unique cultural, social, and historical variants. For this to happen, the nature of that which is political or that which inspires competition between groups or individuals for power must be acknowledged as existing and influencing socially constructed systems, including education and psychology. Moving from apathy to movement will not happen overnight because systemic apathy is the result of years of neglect, ignorance, and abuse. However, as long as like-minded individuals continue to theorize, anticipate, participate, and advocate for change and the equitable treatment of all persons, there will always be the promise of a more just society.

References

Alim, M., Due, C., & Strelan, P. (2019). Perceptions of forgiveness in response to systemic injustice among Iranian refugees. *Peace and Conflict: Journal of Peace Psychology*, 25(3), 255–258. https://doi.org/10.1037/pac0000355

Au, W. (2013). Hiding behind high-stakes testing: Meritocracy, objectivity and inequality in U.S. education. *International Education Journal: Comparative Perspectives*, 12(2), 7–19.

Ball, S. J., & Olmedo, A. (2013). Care of the self, resistance and subjectivity under neoliberal governmentalities. *Critical Studies in Education, 54*(1), 85–96. https://doi.org/10.1080/17508487.2013.740678

Blader, S. L., & Chen, Y.-R. (2012, January 9). Differentiating the effects of status and power: A justice perspective. *Journal of Personality and Social Psychology.* Advance online publication. https://doi.org/10.1037/a0026651

Brookfield, S. (2002). Overcoming alienation as the practice of adult education: The contribution of Erich Fromm to a critical theory of adult learning and education. *Adult Education Quarterly, 52*(2), 96–111. Retrieved February 26, 2018, from www.uwyo.edu/aded5050/5050unit14/overcomi.pdf

Cameron Kelly, D., & Varghese, R. (2018). Four contexts of institutional oppression: Examining the experiences of Blacks in education, criminal justice and child welfare. *Journal of Human Behavior in the Social Environment, 28*(7), 874–888. https://doi.org/10.1080/10911359.2018.1466751

Cronick, K. (2002). Community, subjectivity, and intersubjectivity. *American Journal of Community Psychology, 30*(4), 529–46. doi:http://dx.doi.org.prescottcollege. idm.oclc.org/10.1023/A:1015860002096

Deutsch, M. (2006). A framework for thinking about oppression and its change. *Social Justice Research, 19*(1), 7–41. https://doi.org/10.1007/s11211-006-9998-3

Fox, D., Prilleltensky, I., & Austin, S. (2009). Critical psychology for social justice: Concerns and dilemmas. In D. Fox, I. Prilleltensky, & S. Austin (Eds.), *Critical psychology: An introduction* (pp. 3–19). Thousand Oaks, CA: Sage.

Freire, P. (2005). *Pedagogy of the oppressed* (M. Bergman Ramos, Trans., 30th Anniversary ed.). New York, NY: Continuum International Publishing Group. (Original work published 1970).

Fromm, E. (1976). *To have or to be.* London: Sphere.

Fromm, E. (2008). *Sane society.* Abingdon: Routledge. (Original work published 1956).

Giroux, H. A., & Giroux, S. S. (2006). Challenging neoliberalism's new world order: The promise of critical pedagogy. *Cultural Studies: Critical Methodologies, 6*(1), 21–32.

Gould, S.J. (1996). *The mismeasure of man.* New York, NY: W.W. Norton & Company.

Gump, J. P. (2010). Reality matters: The shadow of trauma on African American subjectivity. *Journal of Psychoanalytic Psychology, 21*(1), 42–54. https://doi. org/10.1037/a0018639

Hill Collins, P. (1995). The social construction of black feminist thought. In B. Guy-Sheftall (Ed.), *Words of fire: An anthology of African-American feminist thought* (pp. 338–357). New York, NY: New York Press. Retrieved February 26, 2019, from https://ebookcentral.proquest.com/lib/prescottcollege-ebooks/detail.action? docID=1011634

Hook, D., Collins, A., Mkhize, N., Kiguwa, P., Parker, I., & Burman, E. (2004). *Critical psychology.* Cape Town: Juta.

Iverson, S. V. (2007). Camouflaging power and privilege: A critical race analysis of university diversity policies. *Educational Administration Quarterly, 43*(5), 586–611.

Johnston-Goodstar, K., & VeLure Roholt, R. (2017). Our kids aren't dropping out: They're being pushed out: Native American students and racial microaggressions in schools. *Journal of Ethnic and Cultural Diversity in Social Work*, *26*(1–2), 30–47. https://doi.org/10.1080/15313204.2016.1263818

Jung, C. G. (1938). Psychological reflections: A Jung anthology. *Psychological Aspects of the Modern Archetype*, *9*.

Karier, C. J. (1972). Testing for order and control in the corporate liberal state. *Educational Theory*, *22*(Spring), 159–180.

Kelly, M. G. (2013). Foucault, subjectivity, and the technologies of the self. In C. Falzon, T. O'Leary, & J. Sawicky (Eds.), *A companion to Foucault*. Chichester: Wiley-Blackwell.

Kozol, J. (1992). *Savage inequalities: Children in America's schools*. New York, NY: Harper Perennial.

Kukathas, C. (1998). Liberalism and multiculturalism: The politics of indifference. *Political Theory*, *26*(5), 686–699. Retrieved February 26, 2019, from https://eclass. uoa.gr/modules/document/file.php/PRIMEDU143/Kukathas, Liberalism & Multiculturalism.pdf

Lakes, R. D., & Carter, P. A. (2011). Neoliberalism and education: An introduction. *Educational Studies*, *47*, 107–110. https://doi.org/10.1080/00131946.2011.556387

Latane, B., & Darley, J. M. (1969). Bystander "apathy." *American Scientist*, *57*(2), 248–268. Retrieved from www.truthaboutnursing.org/research/orig/latane_and_ darley/bystander_apathy.pdf

Marin, R. S. (1991). Apathy: A neuropsychiatric syndrome. *Journal of Neuropsychiatry and Clinical Neurosciences*, *3*(3), 243–254. https://doi.org/10.1176/jnp. 3.3.243

Marx, K. (1978). *The Marx-Engels reader* (R. C. Tucker, Ed.). New York, NY: W. W. Norton.

Meadows, D. (1997). Places to intervene in a system. *Whole Earth*, *91*(1), 78–84.

Mertens, D. M. (2007). Transformative paradigm: Mixed methods and social justice. *Journal of Mixed Methods Research*, *1*, 212–225. https://doi.org/10.1177/ 1558689807302811

Minh-ha, T. T. (1989). *Woman native other*. Bloomington, IN: Indiana University Press.

Montero, M. (1982). Fundamentos teóricos de la Psicología social comunitaria en Latinoamérica. *AVEPSO*, *5*(1), 15–22.

Novak, M. (2009, December 29). *Social justice: Not what you think it is*. Retrieved April 26, 2019, from www.heritage.org/poverty-and-inequality/report/social-justice-not-what-you-think-it

Perry, T., Steele, C., & Hilliard, A. G., III. (2003). *Young, gifted, and black: Promoting high achievement among African-American students*. Boston, MA: Beacon Press.

Portelli, J., & Konecny, C. P. (2013). Neoliberalism, subversion, and democracy in education. *Encounters on Education*, *14*, 87–97.

Radakovic, R., & Abrahams, S. (2014). Developing a new apathy measurement scale: Dimensional apathy scale. *Psychiatry Research*, *219*(3), 658–663. https:// doi.org/10.1016/j.psychres.2014.06.010

Sharma, S. G. (2009). Justice without power is inefficient, power without justice is tyranny. *SSRN Electronic Journal*. https://doi.org/10.2139/ssrn.1329885

Sheikh, F. A. (2017). Subjectivity, desire and theory: Reading Lacan. *Cogent Arts and Humanities*, *4*, 1–12. https://doi.org/10.1080/23311983.2017.1299565

Sugarman, J. (2015). Neoliberalism and psychological ethics. *Journal of Theoretical and Philosophical Psychology*, *35*(2), 103–116. https://doi.org/10.1037/a0038960

Teo, T. (2015). Critical psychology: A geography of intellectual engagement and resistance. *American Psychologist*, *70*(3), 243–254. https://doi.org/10.1037/a0038727

Thomas, E. F., McGarty, C., & Mavor, K. I. (2009). Transforming "apathy into movement": The role of prosocial emotions in motivating action for social change. *Personality and Social Psychology Review*, *13*, 310–333. https://doi.org/10.1177/1088868309343290

Thrift, E., & Sugarman, J. (2019). What is social justice? Implications for psychology. *Journal of Theoretical and Philosophical Psychology*, *39*(1), 1–17. https://doi.org/10.1037/teo0000097

Van Reekum, R., Stuss, D. T., & Ostrander, L. (2005). Apathy: Why care? *Journal of Neuropsychiatry and Clinical Neurosciences*, *17*(1), 7–19. Retrieved from https://neuro.psychiatryonline.org/doi/full/10.1176/jnp.17.1.7

3 Addressing the Empty Self

Toward Socially Just Subjectivities

Interest in the relationship between psychology and social justice has grown in recent years (Thrift & Sugarman, 2019). This interest has included increasing recognition of the ways that psychology perpetuates and/or challenges injustices as well as the impact of societal factors on what is often considered *individual* psychological well-being. However, there has been less recognition of the impact of psychological well-being—or lack therefore—on societal conditions. Understanding exactly what social justice is, or should be, as well as what the role of psychology should be in issues of social justice, are complicated topics skillfully explored in Thrift and Sugarman's recent article, "What Is Social Justice: Implications for Psychology" (2019). While this project of articulation is important, the current work argues that the modern Western subject is constructed in such a way as to be in chronic conflict with myriad visions of social justice and greater societal well-being. Without addressing the problems of subjectivity, efforts to promote any vision of social justice—both within and beyond psychology—may be deeply hindered.

Individual and societal well-being are often studied separately by separate disciplines. This academic separation simplifies a complex system in order to make study more manageable, however we often forget that this separation is artificial. This forgetting contributes to a real and detrimental division in a naturally holistic system. In order to support effective and meaningful gains in well-being in any area, we argue it is crucial to consider the inherent interrelatedness of subjects and the larger systems which simultaneously produce and are produced by them. We acknowledge, however, that in practice it may remain beneficial for various disciplines, such as psychology, to focus on one level or another more specifically *while maintaining the broader perspective of interrelatedness*. As a discipline which tends to focus more on the individual level, psychology is poised to support radical social change through supporting radical change at the level of the subject.

The following sections explore some of the particular challenges for holistic well-being emerging from problematic modern subjectivities as well as the involvement of psychology in supporting and/or failing to challenge contributing conditions. Emptiness—or a deep sense of lack at the core of our being—has been identified as being a major factor in human struggle and in the construction of subjectivities by fields such as theology, philosophy, and psychology. In fact, Cushman notes that "the empty self has become such a prevalent aspect of our culture that much contemporary psychotherapeutic theory is devoted to its treatment" (1990, p. 604). Without addressing emptiness, alternative subjectivity constructions may still be plagued by the same basic struggles, thereby undermining potential gains. Thus the concept and challenges of emptiness—along with alternative approaches to understanding and working with emptiness—are explored here.

Ultimately this exploration is meant to go beyond critique to generate thought, dialogue, and activity towards change. Therefore, with the caveat that this must ultimately be a collaborative endeavor, preliminary visions for alternative paths through which psychology could support the development of more healthful and just subjectivities are offered. Drawing on an array of wisdom traditions as well as growing empirical evidence, suggested approaches include facilitating greater development of compassion and interconnectivity. Such developments could help us feel less alienated and more connected, aid in healthful meaning making, ease feelings of emptiness, become more attuned to and proactive toward the well-being of others, and ultimately enhance individual, societal, global, and environmental well-being.

Subjectivities, Social Justice, and Psychology

There is growing consensus among critical social and psychological theorists that "contemporary culture has . . . become excessively narcissistic, competitively individualistic, and consumption-focused" (Gruba-McCallister, 2007, p. 183). This culture and the subjects included in it are typically associated with capitalistic, consumeristic, and neoliberal ideologies of the West, however globalization is increasingly leading to the export of both these ideologies and their problematic subjectivities. In addition to individual challenges, such as growing rates of depression, anxiety, and interpersonal struggles, we are also witnessing increasing social and political tensions, decreasing social support, and increasing environmental degradation. This trend is reflected in the 2006 United Nations report indicating a "worldwide dwindling of political commitment in aid of social justice policies and practices" (as cited in Thrift & Sugarman, 2019, p. 3). A growing body of empirical research supports theoretical assertions that qualities associated with modern neoliberal subjectivities—such as materialism, consumerism, individualism, and narcissism—are incompatible (or at least in tension) with beliefs and behaviors supporting social justice (Kasser, Ryan, Couchman, & Sheldon, 2003; Solomon, Greenberg, & Pyszczynski, 2003).

Increasing awareness of the relationship between individual and societal well-being has led to calls for psychologists to consider how societal conditions impact individual well-being and to become advocates of social change in order to improve the social conditions in which individuals exist. Critical psychologies in particular have been strong advocates of the need for social reform in order to support the well-being of individuals. Through collective efforts we have witnessed a number of positive social changes over the past decades; however such progress has also been met with resistance and backlash. Current examples include increasing nationalism and xenophobia, rising rates of hate crimes (Eligon, 2018), efforts to restrict women's health rights, the separation and detention of refugee families (including infants and children), and much more.

A top-down approach to making the world a more socially just place by focusing on overhauling social systems, laws, and policies is certainly needed. And while these systemic changes could theoretically shift subjectivity constructions over time, complementary bottom-up efforts to intentionally support positive changes in subjectivity constructions could contribute to more organic and effective gains in holistic well-being while also minimizing intra- and interpersonal tensions and backlashes. This approach draws on theories which understand particular subjectivities to be locally, socially, and historically constructed rather than fundamental to human nature (Cushman, 1990; Gruba-McCallister, 2007; Sugarman, 2015), with some subjectivities being better suited to individual, societal, or holistic well-being.

If the current neoliberal subjectivities that populate and embody our social systems (and this includes you and me, dear reader) are in fact laden with characteristics such as those associated with hyper-individualism and narcissism, then efforts to promote social justice will necessarily be experienced as antagonistic to our nature and will feel restrictive and oppressive. The prevalence and dominance of these negative qualities are arguably the result of particular neoliberal constructions of subjectivity, however they are often mistaken as being among the most fundamental qualities of human nature. This belief contributes to harm for both individuals and society.

When the larger neoliberal climate in which we live generally understands humans to be fundamentally selfish and greedy (Gruba-McCallister,

2007), our approaches to justice often attempt to operate through force and guilt rather than appeals to our inner goodness. This can be seen in the ways that we police ourselves and each other, with even slight perceived transgressions often bearing serious and devastating consequences. In this environment, even those who consider themselves social justice advocates may live in fear of being brutally "called out" and cast out for the slightest slip of language (Johnson, 2016).

In some ways, social justice movements can be seen as operating at least in part from Kohlberg's pre-conventional level of moral development. Kohlberg identified this as being the first stage of moral development, at which point moral behavior is determined primarily by acts believed to bring either reward or punishment for the actor (Kohlberg & Hersh, 1977). Additionally, while postmodernism and the critical turn have challenged beliefs in absolute truths (coming from science, religions, etc.), we still seem to crave solid ground to stand on—especially with such complex and important issues as morality. In a society that tells us that human nature is essentially selfish and in which we regularly experience being called out for having (often unconsciously) committed some offense against our fellow humans, we yearn for a rule book that will tell us how to think, feel, and behave in every instance. We could then hold ourselves and one another accountable to these rules while also absolving a certain amount of personal responsibility (we are only responsible for following the rules, not for deciding what the moral action should be in each circumstance). Unfortunately, we can get so caught up in the project of articulating and enforcing "justice" that we resort to methods which themselves impair well-being and create harm. Additionally, these sets of rules that we must learn, memorize, and attempt to adhere to in order to be good and just are ever-changing and ever-lengthening, making this rule-based system of morality particularly challenging and disheartening.

Given the construction of neoliberal subjectivities, appealing to other's (and our own) sense of self-preservation rather than deeper senses of social responsibility and empathy seems logical. Unfortunately, it also challenges our abilities to work authentically and effectively on behalf of others, to set our egos aside and wrestle with the messiness of goodness—which rarely follows the neat rules we long for. Alternative approaches to moral and ethical action, such as an ethics of care model, have been argued for by thinkers such as Carol Gilligan and Emmanuel Levinas (Bookman & Aboulafia, 2000). Such approaches involved developing personal relational ethics rather than impersonal universal ethics. While such approaches are necessarily messier and place more responsibility on the actor, they are also more adaptable and authentic, require us to recognize and relate to one another, and decrease the risks of objectifying and dehumanizing the other. Levinas's approach is discussed more in the chapter "'I'm Just Not Woke Enough': The Arising of New Symptoms in a Social Justice Age." However, such approaches may depend on radical shifts in modern subjectivities.

Through contact with various cultural systems, certain human potentialities are strengthened while others are minimized. While humans certainly have capacities for selfishness, anti-sociality, and cruelty, they also have capacities for compassion, altruism, empathy, generosity, love, caring, kindness, and general prosociality (Ricard, 2016; Zaki, 2019). Unfortunately, our current cultural systems tend to nurture the former and inhibit the latter capacities. Psychology, as part of these larger cultural systems, has a well-established and powerful role in the shaping of Western subjectivities. Because of this position, as well as a commitment to facilitating well-being, psychology could play a significant role in nurturing more compassionate, altruistic, and interconnected subjectivities. Psychology could work to promote social justice by appealing to the inherently prosocial qualities existing (even if dormant) within us all. This in turn could organically support radical improvements in individual and societal well-being.

In order to explore the viability of working on the level of subjectivity constructions to support greater social justice and holistic well-being, it is beneficial to first examine the conditions contributing to the construction of modern subjectivities. Thankfully, thorough and insightful examinations of this nature have already been undertaken (Cushman, 1996; Fromm, 1955; Gruba-McCallister, 2007; Loy, 2000; McWilliams, 2010; Shiah, 2016; Sugarman, 2015; Xavier, 2016). A brief overview of such examinations is provided below.

Fromm and Social Character

Erich Fromm's *The Sane Society* (1955/1990) provided one of the first critiques of capitalism and its impacts on psychological well-being. In this work, Fromm undertook something akin to Foucault's later archaeologies of subjectivity, outlining the impact of capitalism on the development and evolution of what Fromm called "social character." Fromm argued that particular character structures are constructed within capitalist systems and that these structures are inherently unhealthy and prone to a wide range of psychological struggles, including depression, anxiety, alienation, and narcissism. Interestingly, Fromm also turned his diagnostic lens on society itself, suggesting that societies which fail to support the well-being and flourishing of the individuals within them can themselves be considered "sick" and that widespread psychological struggles can be understood as valuable symptoms toward diagnosing illnesses of society.

Fromm argued humans feel an inherent sense of emptiness and believed that the world's spiritual traditions, as well as much of culture, largely serve to assuage this emptiness (Gruba-McCallister, 2007). These ameliorative traditions and cultures were seriously challenged by the rise of capitalism. In the resulting materialistic, atheistic, alienated, and culturally atrophied environments, Fromm argued that individuals necessarily turned to capitalism and consumerism—the only options left to them—to provide self-worth, meaning making, values, cultural guidance, connection, and more. The focus of capitalism, however, is not to meet our needs but to produce profit, and meeting desires has proven both more profitable and easier than meeting needs.

Unfortunately, we often desire things that are detrimental to our well-being (Grant, 2017). Thus our attempts to assuage emptiness through capitalistic and consumeristic means creates deeper feelings of emptiness and carries us further away from that which would actually soothe our souls (Fromm, 1955/1990). Our relationship with fast food provides an apt metaphor for this approach to addressing emptiness. When we consume large amounts of fast and processed foods to satiate our hunger on a regular basis, we may feel a certain kind of fullness. However, these foods contain little of what our bodies actually need. Because these foods are so readily available, convenient, cheap, and appeal to our primal desires for sugar, salt, and fat, we may neglect to seek out other foods while becoming slowly and unknowingly deficient in vital nutrients. In an attempt to meet these deficiencies, our bodies tell us to eat more, at which point we go back to the fast-food restaurant and order twice as many cheeseburgers, thus creating an increasingly damaging cycle.

Fromm was aware of the challenges to agency and choice that individuals face within capitalist societies (or any societies), but he also believed that it was possible for individuals to reorient their focus toward healthier modes of being. The first step in this process is awareness—waking up to our situation, to our alienation and emptiness (Fromm, 1955/1990). Once this occurs, we can begin to consider alternate actions within the circumstances in which we exist. This echoes the liberatory power of Paulo Freire's *conscientization*, "the process whereby people attain an insightful awareness of the socio-economic, political, and cultural circumstances which affect their lives as well as their potential capacity to transform that social reality" (Prilleltensky, 1990, p. 311). We may not be able to fundamentally alter our external circumstances (at least not today), but we do have varying degrees of freedom for how we live within and challenge them.

Cushman and the Empty Self

Philip Cushman has also provided extensive psychological explorations of the development of subjectivities within modern capitalist societies (1990, 1996). Cushman's basic argument is that capitalism both produces our sense of emptiness through creating losses in community, culture, connections, identity, and systems of meaning making and then exploits this emptiness for profit.

Cushman identifies two primary profitable industries which act to treat, or at least manage the discomfort, of what he calls the "empty self": advertising and psychotherapy (1990). Advertising works with consumerism to treat the empty self by providing desirable lifestyles, identities, beliefs, cultures, connections, and meaning that one can symbolically consume and thereby fill up the emptiness with perceived substance (Cushman, 1990). While this may give us continuing hope that happiness is right around the corner, consumption never quite delivers on its promises. In fact, research indicates that consumeristic and materialist attitudes and practices are more often negatively correlated with happiness and well-being and positively correlated with a number of psychological and emotional challenges (De Graff, Wann, & Naylor, 2002; Kasser et al., 2003; Leonard, 2010; Schor, 1999; Solberg, Diener, & Robinson, 2003). As Fromm noted, a cycle is produced in which emptiness leads to consumption, which leads to greater feelings of emptiness and the feeling that we must be doing something wrong.

Psychotherapy, Cushman argues, attempts to treat the empty self by focusing on building up and reifying the ego in part through the therapist—acting as a kind of guru—providing identities, values, connections, meaning, and so forth for the client to build on (Cushman, 1990, 1996). This approach may offer some rudimentary relief for individuals. However, because both psychological theories and therapists have absorbed capitalistic and consumeristic values, psychotherapy often contributes to the construction of overly individualistic and self-serving subjectivities, with "specific psychological boundaries, an internal locus of control, and a wish to manipulate the external world for its own personal ends" (Cushman, 1990, p. 600). The narcissistic self which emerges continues to suffer from a deep sense of emptiness while also producing additional intrapersonal, interpersonal, and societal suffering.

Neoliberal Subjectivities

More recent explorations of modern subjectivities are moving toward examinations of the effects of neoliberal ideologies on subjectivity constructions. In *Neoliberalism and Psychological Ethics*, Sugarman (2015) argues that neoliberalism—associated with conditions such as mobilized workforces, self-branding, consumer-based identity formation, extreme self-reliance, and increasing disregard for socially oriented ethics and values—is enhancing individualistic and narcissistic attitudes as people increasingly feel they must sell themselves on the work and social markets. Additionally, neoliberal values directly attack social relations and responsibilities, promoting the message that happiness depends upon

> [extricating] ourselves from a legacy of interdependencies and the misbegotten beliefs that perpetuate them: the importance of mutual commitments, social cohesion, and collective responsibility . . . an overdependence on habits acquired by conforming to conventional patterns of social interaction and communal life.
>
> (Sugarman, 2015, p. 109)

As Gruba-McCallister (2007) notes, "the characteristics of selfishness, greed, and egotism [are not only] valued, [they] are seen as innate to human nature" (p. 186). This view makes it difficult for critiques of these characteristics to gain any ground and difficult to pass laws and policies in opposition to them—for instance, those that aim to limit freedoms on pursuits of wealth and personal success. Additionally, this view of human nature has been largely internalized within and (re)produced by psychology, causing psychological theories and practices to defend and even work to strengthen these characteristics.

In this culture of hyper-individualism, happiness is believed to come from the pursuit of hedonic, desire-based self-interests and success with little regard for impacts on the well-being of others and the planet. In this climate, social justice projects become particularly susceptible to self-serving interests. We want to be successful and righteous in our social justice endeavors. This can cause us to condemn others in order to boost our own egos. It can also cause us to become overly attached to predetermined outcomes as markers of success and inhibit our abilities to hear the voices of those we claim to be advocating for if they contradict our own projects. Additionally, it can lead to defensiveness about our own involvement with systems of oppression. Finally, this use of social justice work to boost our egos means that we need injustices to continue in order to continue to feel good about ourselves for fighting against them. Aspects of this challenge are explored elsewhere here in the chapters "Killing the Other: Obsessionality in Cognitive Science and Diversity Initiatives" and "'I'm Just Not Woke Enough': The Arising of New Symptoms in a Social Justice Age."

The following section explores some of the ways that psychology has been complicit in the production and maintenance of capitalistic and neoliberal ideologies and their associated problematic subjectivities.

Problematic Contributions From Psychology

Many have argued that psychology has been deeply implicated in the creation and maintenance of consumeristic, capitalistic, neoliberal, and "empty" subjectivities that are largely incompatible with both individual and societal well-being as well as social justice (Fromm, 1955; Gruba-McCallister, 2007; Sugarman, 2015; Xavier, 2016). One of the major problematic contributions from psychology has been an overemphasis on the individual—with both pathologies and their cures located at the level of the individual—along with a general lack of consideration for the role of society and social factors in individual struggles (Cushman, 1996; Gruba-McCallister, 2007; Shiah, 2016; Sugarman, 2015). A number of sub-disciplines, such as critical, community, and liberation psychologies, have emerged which specifically critique this individual emphasis and attempt to highlight the role of societies and communities in challenging or supporting mental health. Other sub-disciplines, such as transpersonal psychology and ecopsychology, also recognize the problems of overemphasizing the individual and failing to consider both societal contexts as well as our deep embeddedness and interconnections with one another, nature, and spirit (broadly defined). However, these perspectives still remain at the periphery of mainstream psychology.

Absorbing movements toward personal empowerment from humanistic and positive psychologies, mainstream psychology has also become increasingly aligned with neoliberal ideologies, including "moral injunctions to work on the self to attain greater autonomy, to accept responsibility for one's choices and circumstances, to strive to realize one's potential, and to increase one's quality of life" (Sugarman, 2015, p. 108). While all of this sounds positive and empowering at first glance, it places a great deal of pressure on individuals to make themselves "happy." This can lead to denying or repressing uncomfortable but important emotions in ourselves. It can also impact our attitudes and behaviors toward the struggles of others, causing us to see their struggles as their fault and additionally causing us to distance ourselves from them, lest they infect us with their lack of happiness. This all makes it very hard for us to give and receive much needed support when life is at its most challenging, and it also robs us of the meaningful growth and connections which challenge can nourish (Bennett, 2019). Equally important, placing the responsibility of well-being solely on individuals obscures larger societal, cultural, and historical conditions that contribute to individual struggle or well-being and ultimately protects unhealthy and unjust systems from criticism. As Gruba-McCallister (2007) notes, "failing to recognize the role of oppression in contributing to psychological dysfunction leads to blaming the victim and obfuscating the need to question radically the unjust social arrangements that need to be corrected in order to promote human well-being" (p. 183). We deny our suffering even to ourselves, and if we do manage to acknowledge it, we are told it is our own fault and our own responsibility to fix—and then directed to the nearest therapist who is more than willing to help us look within for the source of our suffering.

In addition to this resistance to holding and exploring struggle in ourselves and others, psychology also contributes to the "administered lack" of psychological success. The concept of administered lack has been discussed primarily in the context of advertising and consumerism. Desire for an object or experience is produced by mere exposure to the thing to be desired (Gunderson, 2016). For instance, I may have no prior desire for a particular new piece of technology—let's say an upgraded smartphone. Then, I encounter that item through an advertisement or a store or friend, and a lack is created where there had not been one previously. Now I *lack* the new phone (despite having a perfectly good phone already), and that lack produces desire. We argue that psychology does something similar by propagating visions of happiness and personal well-being/success that may not only be unattainable but fundamentally unrealistic and idealistic. It is no longer enough to be free from pathology; we cannot consider ourselves successful if we are merely functioning. "Failing" to reach an ideal state of health, happiness, and self-actualization has now become pathologized, with the blame and responsibility almost always falling on the individual. We are then left with the omnipresent feeling that we lack something we *should* have, and that it's our fault. Psychology contributes to this sense of lack, which leads to increased individualistic and narcissistic traits, increased greed and consumption, and decreased concern for the well-being of others. It then promises to fix our suffering and feelings of emptiness—or, rather, show us how to fix ourselves—for a fee. This again deflects attention away from larger societal problems. As Fromm noted (1955/1990), individual struggles can be understood as symptoms and thus valuable indicators of systemic societal illness, however when these symptoms are misdiagnosed as individual we not only miss opportunities for larger change but actually prohibit societal evolution toward greater well-being.

The concept of lack, or emptiness, as a source of suffering and struggle has played a prominent role in psychological theories throughout the history of the discipline (Gruba-McCallister, 2007; Loy, 2000). However, the broader context in which this emptiness exists has rarely been considered. Cushman notes, "the patient is diagnosed as empty and fragmented, usually without addressing the sociocultural predicament that caused emptiness and fragmentation" (Cushman, 1990, p. 601). Whether emptiness is inherent to human nature or constructed through societal conditions, it seems clear that modern capitalistic and neoliberal ideals present in society and by extension in psychology at least contribute to—and exploit—this emptiness (Gruba-McCallister, 2007). Psychotherapy often attempts "to treat the modern [empty] self by reinforcing the very qualities of the self that have initially caused the problem: it's autonomous, bounded, masterful nature" (Cushman, 1990, p. 601). However, there are other ways to both understand and address emptiness. The following section outlines some of these alternative approaches.

Alternative Approaches to the Empty Self

As we have seen, a number of psychological theorists have contributed to examinations of emptiness and narcissism in relation to capitalism and later neoliberalism. Some, like Cushman, see emptiness as a condition of subjectivities arising from their construction within particular societal systems (i.e., capitalism), while others, like Fromm, understand emptiness as an inherent aspect of the human condition which capitalism then aggravates and exploits. Examinations of emptiness, however, are not limited to psychology, nor are they limited to modern capitalist societies. In fact, emptiness has been a focus of inquiry and concern throughout the ages, particularly within theological and philosophical traditions. Exploring these broader understandings of emptiness can provide a fuller picture of how it relates to modern society and how we might be able to address it in ways which promote more holistic well-being.

Emptiness as Divine Lack

Many religious traditions view emptiness as a meaningful vacuum arising from our disconnection with the divine. This emptiness propels us to seek self-transcendent (re)connections with the divine (both directly and through connections with one another, nature, etc.; Gruba-McCallister, 2007). From this perspective, attempting to fill up or cover over this emptiness with consumer goods, inflated egos, and so on distracts us from hearing the deeper call for connection and transcendence and leads us further from those essential connections. While there are diverse beliefs and practices among different religious traditions, many share prescriptions for humility, compassion, service, contemplation, and prayer, all of which act to minimize the focus on the self and support self-transcendent connections.

Emptiness as Existential Condition

A more secular but related understanding of emptiness comes from existential and humanistic traditions. This understanding is reflected in Fromm's writing. Similar to Buddhism, this view typically understands emptiness to be a primary construction of human consciousness and an unavoidable part of the human experience (though it is aggravated and exploited in certain societal conditions, such as those associated with capitalism). This emptiness is thought to both arise from and contribute to existential anxieties around isolation, mortality, meaninglessness, and so forth. Once again, focusing on highly individualistic, hedonic, material, desire-driven pursuits is believed to antagonize the feelings of emptiness and alienation. However, echoing religious perspectives, existential and humanistic traditions commonly see emptiness as at least in service of—if not existing for—higher human experiences including deep connections (with one another, nature, humanity, etc.), compassion, love, meaning making, self-actualization, peak experiences, and self-transcendence, and further recommend investing in these experiences as a way to healthfully deal with the sense of emptiness.

Emptiness as Misidentification With Self

Buddhist thought offers particularly rich and well-developed theories of emptiness and its relationship to subjectivity and well-being. Emptiness is identified as arising from the misidentification with the self (or rather with constructed selves/subjectivities) and attributes much of human suffering to this misidentification (Loy, 2000; Rahula, 1974; Shiah, 2016). This "false" sense of self emerges as a primary construction through our being in the world (our sensations, perceptions, thoughts, contact with others, language, etc.)—the mix that goes into making up our particular human consciousness. We experience things and understand that they are different from what others experience, and we feel that there must be a solid, real, and enduring "I" at the center of this experiencing (particularly the experience of desire). Buddhist theories generally recognize the necessity of a *functional* sense of self which acts as an organizing principle to help us make meaningful sense of our experiences and navigate our existence. The problem lies in our understanding this functional self to be a distinct and bounded entity rather than an organizing principle—a happening. When we go looking for the "I," it is ultimately nowhere to be found. This, it is believed, leads to a deep sense of emptiness or lack which is at the root of all other desires. Similar insights are echoed in a number of existential and phenomenological philosophies, as well as by psychoanalytic theorists such as Lacan and Zizek. Buddhist thought often differs, however, in its assertion that emptiness can be dissolved rather than merely dealt with, however "healthfully." The empty self may be a primary construction, but it is still a construction, and as such it can be deconstructed and reconstructed in more holistic and less empty ways (Loy, 2000).

Echoing the religious traditions discussed above, the Buddhist prescription for addressing—or in this case transforming—the empty self is to minimize the focus on and importance of the self rather than maximize or reify it (Loy, 2000; Shiah, 2016). This is thought to reduce suffering in part because a strong (mis)identification with the self as separate and bounded blocks our ability to understand and experience our deep interconnectivity with all that is. The existential angst associated with isolation, mortality, and meaninglessness is thought to arise from this misunderstanding of the self as separate from the larger whole, and investments in focusing on and reifying the self, particularly through pursuing hedonic desires, only serve to deepen our disconnections and increase feelings of emptiness. Recommendations for reconstructing the self—or recognizing the self as a process and interdependent happening—often involve practices aimed at increasing feelings of compassion and interconnectivity, becoming more attuned to the direct flow of experiences, and intentionally "starving out" the unhealthy aspects of ego by refraining from overindulgence in hedonic desires/pleasures (Shiah, 2016).

Emptiness as Social Construction

Finally, a fourth understanding of emptiness, represented in Cushman's work (1990, 1996) among other constructionists, is that the empty self is a particular type of subjectivity constructed under certain conditions—such as those experienced in capitalistic and neoliberal societies. As described earlier, this sense of emptiness is thought to occur when societal conditions limit the existence of and/or access to connections, traditions, and culture capable of contributing to a more connected, less alienated, and more meaning-laden subjectivity. While this view is not exactly normative, it does suggest that certain subjectivities are healthier (i.e., produce more individual and societal well-being/happiness and less suffering) than others. From this perspective, attempting to bolster the self by shoring up the ego with material goods, hedonic experiences, branded identities, and so forth increases our feelings of emptiness. We are taught to believe that investing in these pursuits will bring happiness. The failure of this approach and the lack of knowledge of any other approach to happiness— along with the unrelenting demand to be happy—can lead to an increasing sense of discomfort and hopelessness. Additionally, as has been mentioned elsewhere, this approach causes us to be cut off from other experiences that could nurture a "healthy" subjectivity. Recommendations from this perspective include investing in meaningful relationships and connections, developing compassion, engaging in service to others, finding meaning- ful (non-alienating) work, and so on (Gruba-McCallister, 2007)—pursuits which serve once again to shift attention away from the self and facilitate self-transcendent connections.

Quieting the Self: Compassion, Interconnectivity, and Transcendence

While these approaches to understanding and working with emptiness dif- fer, there are also striking similarities. First, each views overly individu- alistic and self-serving orientations as producing and/or antagonizing the suffering associated with emptiness. Second, each of these traditions has, in various forms, attempted to hold society accountable for creating, aggravat- ing, or exploiting emptiness. And finally, each views quieting/minimizing the ego and shifting attention outward through facilitating compassion, ser- vice, awareness and experiences of interconnectivity, and some form of self- transcendence as healthful and effective ways of addressing or dissolving emptiness. These views are increasingly being supported by research from within psychology and beyond (Bauer & Wayment, 2008; Pollan, 2018; Ricard, 2007, 2016).

Compassion seems to ease the discomfort of the empty self in several ways. First, practicing compassion helps us to shift our attention outward and away from the self. Because so much of our reality is what we attend to, this shift can offer a form of self-transcendence. Arthur Deikman (2000) draws on this in his book chapter, "Service as a Way of Knowing." Deik- man argues that we typically spend most of our time attending to the voice and needs of the "survival self," and that this contributes to and magnifies the image of the self as separate, bounded, and always lacking. When we shift our focus to others, and specifically to how we can be of service to oth- ers, "self-interest and self-concern subside and disappear as what-is-called- for takes over" (Deikman, 2000, p. 313). As discussed earlier, countless religious, spiritual, and philosophical traditions have identified excessive self-focus as a common source of suffering and self-transcendence as a common source of well-being.

Second, fostering feelings of compassion seems to also foster feelings of courage, joy, and meaning and to decrease feelings of fear, alienation, and unhappiness (Ricard, 2007, 2016). In addition to wisdom teachings and anecdotal/experiential support, empirical research has shown neurological support for the benefits of compassion—including increased joy and decreased sadness—and for the differences between experiences of empathy and compassion (Ekman, Davidson, Ricard, & Wallace, 2005; Lutz, Brefczynski-Lewis, Johnstone, & Davidson, 2008; Peters & Calvo, 2014; Ricard, 2007). While empathy can leave us feeling overwhelmed and helpless, compassion seems to nourish our energy and well-being. Compassion allows us to maintain understanding of and boundaries between our own emotions and those of others while also motivating us to take action on behalf of others. Additionally, our attention to helping others brings *what we have to offer* into focus, helping us to feel the richness of our gifts and abilities, which in turn helps us to feel secure, competent, and less lacking. Anyone who has ever acted on behalf of a loved one has likely experienced the surprising wellspring of strength and courage that so often arises in such situations. Attending to and acting on behalf of the well-being of others can also help us to feel more connected and contribute to a sense of meaning, purpose, and accomplishment.

Relatedly, interconnectivity can help transform feelings of emptiness by negating the experience of the self as separate, bounded, and finite. Realizing our deep interconnectedness with all that is—with one another, nature, and the universe—again helps to shift attention away from our small self and towards something larger and transcendent. We see that our actions, our joys and sorrows, our struggles and accomplishments, and our very survival are not ours alone but are intrinsically interconnected and interdependent with that of others. In order for interconnectivity to have meaningful impacts on our constructed subjectivities, however, it is not enough to merely *understand* our interconnectedness with all that is; we must have *experiences* of interconnectivity which fundamentally reshape our sense of self (Ricard, 2007). Experiencing our interconnectivity on a deep level can inspire feelings of awe. Awe involves the experience of encountering incomprehensible vastness which often produces new understandings of the world and ourselves (Keltner & Haidt, 2003). We may experience a kind of awe through our awareness of interconnectivity when we consider, for example, that the water in our own bodies came to us on its journey through oceans, rivers, thunderstorms, oak trees, earthworms, and even dinosaurs, and it will continue this journey after its time with us. Like compassion, experiences of awe have been found to contribute to both personal well-being (Rudd, Vohs, & Aaker, 2012) and prosociality (Piff, Dietze, Feinberg, Stancato, & Keltner, 2015).

As we have seen, emptiness is implicated in not only individual but also societal suffering and injustice. Psychology already has a long history of recognizing and working with emptiness as well as an increasing interest in societal well-being and social justice. With alternative insights into modern subjectivities and emptiness—including those presented earlier—psychology could avoid the past traps of contributing to the problems associated with emptiness and modern subjectivities and could work to support the development of healthier subjectivities.

Compassion and interconnectivity provide just two examples we are familiar with that could easily be supported by psychology and its many subfields. Emphasizing the values of compassion and interconnectivity and developing research and practices to support these experiences in people's daily lives, workplaces, schools, and so forth could nourish the development of less empty subjectivities more conducive to social justice and holistic well-being.

New Paths for Psychology

The seemingly perennial recognition of emptiness throughout time and tradition suggests that emptiness may be a struggle which goes beyond our modern times and in fact may contribute to many of the harmful conditions associated with our present society. Capitalism did not emerge from nothing, nor was it bestowed upon us by some external power. As with all socioeconomic and political systems, capitalism is a product of human creation and thus theoretically both reflects and serves us in some way. Buddhist philosopher David Loy (2015) attributes the challenges of capitalism to the three poisons: ignorance, greed, and aggression. Within Buddhist thought, these three poisons are believed to arise from the emptiness of the misidentified self discussed earlier. Loy argues that without addressing these poisons, and ultimately the emptiness behind them, any system we create (along with the subjectivities which emerge from these systems) will necessarily be shaped by them—whether this system is capitalism, socialism, communism, anarchism, or something entirely new. While beliefs in inherent human sin or selfishness often produce pessimistic visions of what is possible for us, the understanding of the three poisons offers hope. These struggles may be primary, but they are not fundamental. We can, Loy (2015) argues, loosen our sense of emptiness and therefore the strength and influence of the poisons.

Societal conditions could theoretically support such changes, but as these societal conditions are produced by us and shaped by our inner conditions, we must work from both levels (societal and individual) simultaneously to create meaningful progress toward holistic well-being.

The broad field of psychology, with its many sub-disciplines, has become an incredibly powerful force in both society and in individual lives. The reach of psychological theories, research, and practice extends to government and politics, education, economics, business and management, law enforcement, culture and entertainment, and more (Sugarman, 2015). We encounter psychological knowledge in our everyday lives through books, films, blogs, psychotherapy, social media, and the general psychology-saturated culture we swim in. This level of power and reach is rare, met only perhaps by the power and reach of religion and advertising in modern culture. It has been argued here and elsewhere that psychology is already having a profound impact on the construction and maintenance of modern subjectivities—often reflecting unhealthy neoliberal values such as extreme individualism and narcissism—and that these subjectivities have been connected to individual and societal suffering and socially unjust beliefs and behaviors.

If psychology—and this is an important if—takes up as its goal the reduction of suffering and enhancement of well-being for all, it must recognize the implicit capitalistic and neoliberal values it has absorbed and further take responsibility for its influence on subjectivity constructions. We argue that psychology is in need of a fundamental revolution, a fundamental reorientation away from being "architects of adjustment" and toward being "agents of sociopolitical change" (Sugarman, 2015, p. 115). There is already a movement underway—represented most strongly in the current of critical psychology—to do just this. But it is crucial to this project that we focus on holistic change. Without addressing the inseparable interconnectivity between individuals and societies, our efforts in either domain will remain limited. Without examining the subjectivities who are tasked with living out the change we seek, meaningful and lasting gains in social justice and societal well-being—as well as individual well-being—may be undermined by subjectivities incapable of living out these visions.

One way that psychology could support a more just world would be to focus on theoretical and empirical explorations into the values and subjectivity constructions that best promote not only individual but also societal well-being, and to consciously reject the promotion of values which fail to serve *either* of these levels. Such work could yield valuable knowledge that would spread throughout the far reaches of psychology and eventually have the same level of impact on subjectivity constructions that we currently see, while producing radically healthier and more just subjectivities. We believe this work can and should be taken up in every area of psychology, including social and critical psychologies, cognitive and neuro-psychologies, industrial-organizational psychology, educational psychology, theoretical and philosophical psychologies, positive psychology, psychotherapeutic psychology, and beyond.

While this work would necessarily take many forms, there are already some models to draw from in existential/humanistic, theoretical/philosophical, transpersonal, eco-, contemplative, and even positive psychologies (to name a few). Early research on the benefits of quieting the ego (Bauer & Wayment, 2008; Kesebir, 2014), developing compassion and altruism (Ekman et al., 2005; Ricard, 2007, 2016), and strengthening relationships, connections, and interconnectivity is already showing promise for both individual and social well-being (Grant, 2018; Kesebir, 2014). Transpersonal psychology (and by extension ecopsychology) offers particularly hopeful models for the future as it already "represents a value-laden responsible *moral science of action* rather than a value-free and determinist *natural science of behavior*" (Daniels, 2015, p. 24), is dedicated to empirical investigation and support for theories and practices, seeks "to tackle the wider social problems such as alienation, 'moral decline,' rampant materialism, and ecological destruction" (Daniels, 2015, p. 39), and has established a growing body of knowledge around the individual and social benefits of compassion and interconnectivity.

This work must start with ourselves, however, for how are we to nurture the development of healthier and more just subjectivities if we are still operating from subjectivities deeply reflective of neoliberal beliefs, attitudes, and values? Such shifts in our own subjectivities could produce beneficial shifts in the psychotherapeutic "treatment" of the empty self identified by Cushman, taking therapy beyond adjusting clients to an insane society to facilitating much deeper healing. Beyond therapy, such personal shifts would have an impact on the research projects we choose to engage in, the educational theories and recommendations we put forth, the policies we support, and the countless books and blogs and podcasts and TV shows and films we contribute to. This kind of commitment to dealing with emptiness (our own and others) differently, to supporting *holistic* wellness, and to creating a culture which nourishes our positive capacities for things like compassion, interconnectivity, and transcendence could contribute greatly to a profound and radical (r)evolutionary transformation toward a better world.

While the path may not be clear, the call for psychology to become more involved in and responsible for the values and subjectivities it propagates is. The current work has hopefully added to this call and provided fodder for further conversation around our contributions to challenges facing individual and societal well-being and social justice, as well as how to move forward differently. It is our hope that this work will inspire the generation of new ideas as to how psychology can become more intentionally involved in the facilitation of social justice and subjectivities capable of living it out.

References

Bauer, J. J., & Wayment, H. A. (2008). The psychology of the quiet ego. In *Transcending self-interest: Psychological explorations of the quiet ego* (pp. 7–19). Washington, DC: American Psychological Association.

Bennett, V. S. (2019). *The danger in fake positivity and spiritual bypassing.* Retrieved September 21, 2019, from https://humanparts.medium.com/the-danger-in-fake-positivity-and-spiritual-bypassing-c202040b8dd3

Bookman, M., & Aboulafia, M. (2000). Ethics of care revisited: Gilligan and Levinas. *Philosophy Today, 44,* 169.

Cushman, P. (1990). Why the self is empty: Toward a historically situated psychology. *American Psychologist, 45*(5), 599–611.

Cushman, P. (1996). *Constructing the self, constructing America: A cultural history of psychotherapy.* Cambridge, MA: Da Capo Press.

Daniels, M. (2015). Traditional roots, history, and evolution of the transpersonal perspective. In H. L. Friedman & G. Hartelius (Eds.), *The Wiley-Blackwell handbook of transpersonal psychology* (pp. 23–43). Malden, MA: Wiley-Blackwell.

De Graff, J., Wann, D., & Naylor, T. H. (2002). *Affluenza: The all-consuming epidemic.* San Francisco, CA: Berrett-Koehler.

Deikman, A. J. (2000). Service as a way of knowing. In T. Hart, P. L. Nelson, & K. Puhakka (Eds.), *Transpersonal knowing: Exploring the horizon of consciousness* (pp. 303–318). Albany, NY: State University of New York Press.

Ekman, P., Davidson, R. J., Ricard, M., & Wallace, B. A. (2005). Buddhist and psychological perspectives on emotions and well-being. *Current Directions in Psychological Science, 14*(2), 59–63.

Eligon, J. (2018). Hate crimes increase for the third consecutive year, F.B.I. reports. *New York Times.* Retrieved from www.nytimes.com/2018/11/13/us/hate-crimes-fbi-2017.html

Fromm, E. (1955/1990). *The sane society.* New York: Holt Paperbacks.

Grant, A. S. (2017). What exactly are we trying to accomplish? The role of desire in transhuman visions. In C. Mercer & T. J. Trothen (Eds.), *Religion and human enhancement: Death, values, and morality* (pp. 121–138). New York, NY: Palgrave Macmillan.

Grant, A. S. (2018). *Beyond buffering: An empirical investigation of the interconnective self-construal as a mediator in existential death anxiety.* ProQuest Information & Learning. (2018-48576-011).

Gruba-McCallister, F. (2007). Narcissism and the empty self: To have or to be. *Journal of Individual Psychology, 63*(2), 182–192.

Gunderson, R. (2016). The will to consume: Schopenhauer and consumer society. *Critical Horizons, 17*(3/4), 376–389. https://doi.org/10.1080/14409917.2016.1190181

Johnson, M. Z. (2016, May 6). *6 signs your call-out isn't actually about accountability*. Retrieved September 12, 2019, from https://everydayfeminism.com/2016/05/call-out-accountability/

Kasser, T., Ryan, R. M., Couchman, C. E., & Sheldon, K. M. (2003). Materialistic values: Their causes and consequences. In A. D. Kanner & T. Kasser (Eds.), *Psychology and consumer culture: The struggle for a good life in a materialistic world* (pp. 11–28). Washington, DC: American Psychological Association.

Keltner, D., & Haidt, J. (2003). Approaching awe, a moral, spiritual, and aesthetic emotion. *Cognition and Emotion, 17*(2), 297–314. https://doi.org/10.1080/02699930302297

Kesebir, P. (2014). A quiet ego quiets death anxiety: Humility as an existential anxiety buffer. *Journal of Personality and Social Psychology, 106*(4), 610–623. https://doi.org/10.1037/a0035814

Kohlberg, L., & Hersh, R. H. (1977). Moral development: A review of the theory. *Theory into Practice, 16*(2), 53–59. https://doi.org/10.1080/00405847709542675

Leonard, A. (2010). *The story of stuff*. New York, NY: Free Press.

Loy, D. (2000). *Lack and transcendence: The problem of death and life in psychotherapy, existentialism, and Buddhism*. Amherst, NY: Humanity Books.

Loy, D. (2015). *A new Buddhist path: Enlightenment, evolution, and ethics in the modern world*. Somerville, MA: Wisdom.

Lutz, A., Brefczynski-Lewis, J., Johnstone, T., & Davidson, R. J. (2008). Regulation of the neural circuitry of emotion by compassion meditation: Effects of meditative expertise. *PLoS One, 3*(3), e1897. https://doi.org/10.1371%2Fjournal.pone.0001897

McWilliams, S. A. (2010). Inherent self, invented self, empty self: Constructivism, Buddhism, and psychotherapy. *Counseling and Values, 55*, 79–100.

Peters, D., & Calvo, R. (2014). Compassion vs. Empathy: Designing for resilience. *Interactions, 21*(5), 49–53.

Piff, P. K., Dietze, P., Feinberg, M., Stancato, D. M., & Keltner, D. (2015). Awe, the small self, and prosocial behavior. *Journal of Personality and Social Psychology, 108*(6), 883–899. https://doi.org/10.1037/pspi0000018

Pollan, M. (2018). *How to change your mind: What the new science of psychedelics teaches us about consciousness, dying, addiction, depression, and transcendence*. New York, NY: Penguin Press.

Prilleltensky, I. (1990). Enhancing the social ethics of psychology: Toward a psychology at the service of social change. *Canadian Psychology/Psychologie Canadienne, 31*(4), 310–319. https://doi.org/10.1037/h0078954

Rahula, W. (1974). *What the Buddha taught: Revised and expanded edition with texts from Suttas and Dhammapada*. New York, NY: Grove Press.

Ricard, M. (2007). *Happiness: A guide to developing life's most important skill* (J. Browner, Trans.). New York, NY: Little, Brown.

Ricard, M. (2016). *Altruism: The power of compassion to change yourself and the world*. New York, NY: Little, Brown.

Rudd, M., Vohs, K. D., & Aaker, J. (2012). Awe expands people's perception of time, alters decision making, and enhances well-being. *Psychological Science*, *23*(10), 1130–1136. https://doi.org/10.1177/0956797612438731

Schor, J. (1999). *The overspent American*. New York, NY: Harper Perennial.

Shiah, Y.-J. (2016). From self to nonself: The nonself theory. *Frontiers in Psychology*, *7*(124), 1–12. https://doi.org/10.3389/fpsyg.2016.00124

Solberg, E. G., Diener, E., & Robinson, C. E. (2003). Why are materialists less satisfied? In A. D. Kanner & T. Kasser (Eds.), *Psychology and consumer culture: The struggle for a good life in a materialistic world* (pp. 29–48). Washington, DC: American Psychological Association.

Solomon, S., Greenberg, J., & Pyszczynski, T. A. (2003). Lethal consumption: Death denying materialism. In A. D. Kanner & T. Kasser (Eds.), *Psychology and consumer culture: The struggle for a good life in a materialistic world* (pp. 127–146). Washington, DC: American Psychological Association.

Sugarman, J. (2015). Neoliberalism and psychological ethics. *Journal of Theoretical and Philosophical Psychology*, *35*(2), 103–116. https://doi.org/10.1037/a0038960

Thrift, E., & Sugarman, J. (2019). What is social justice? Implications for psychology. *Journal of Theoretical and Philosophical Psychology*, *39*(1), 1–17. https://doi.org/10.1037/teo0000097

Xavier, M. (2016). Subjectivity under consumerism: The totalization of the subject as a commodity. *Psicologia & Sociedade*, *28*(2), 207–216. https://doi.org/10.1590/1807-03102016v28n2p207

Zaki, J. (2019). *The war for kindness: Building empathy in a fractured world*. New York, NY: Crown.

4 Cognitive Science, Obsessionality, and Diversity and Inclusion

The purpose of this book has been to consider social justice within the context of the discipline of psychology, with a concerted interest in the role of subjectivity, asking what constitutes a socially just subject. By demonstrating how psychology has participated in the construction of subjectivities that both empower and oppress marginalized individuals, we have suggested that psychology has always been implicated in social justice concerns. Critical psychology has been an important tool in addressing the discipline's contributions to the marginalization of oppressed people as well as the ways in which it has paved paths for social justice initiatives within and outside of the discipline.

We would like to turn our focus slightly to consider how psychological discourses have permeated popular society and become constituted in contemporary neoliberal capitalist discourses, specifically those which privilege a cognitivist perspective of the subject, in order to consider the implications this has on social justice praxes. While it has already been previously discussed the ways in which neoliberalism has constituted the contemporary subject as an empty self, we would like to focus even more specifically on the subject of cognitive sciences as being the subject of neoliberal capitalism and the implications this has on trying to envision solutions to social justice problems. The question then becomes not only whether or not the contemporary subject is suitable to address social justice concerns, but also whether social justice concerns as articulated in certain paradigms are inevitably the product of neoliberal capitalism. This is not to say that a concern about the ethical and compassionate treatment of human subjects regardless of their group memberships is unimportant. Rather, we ask in what ways have these concerns been co-opted and assimilated into the neoliberal project in and of itself. If this is the case, then the implications this has on the actual relationships between groups and encounters with others demarcated by difference must also be addressed.

In referring to social justice concerns, we mean to emphasize here two issues in particular, and we do not claim to be addressing the bevy of issues that activists tackle on a regular basis. The first is concerns about reducing bias in institutional settings, specifically in the workplace. The second is a concern for those who are able to access consumer services. It is important to differentiate here consumer services from those goods and services which are fundamental to well-being, such as medical care, food, and housing. Consumer services pertain to those services a person can partake in for the sake of enjoyment, such as restaurants, movies, and bakeries. In response to concerns about racism, sexism, and homophobia in institutional and commercial contexts, diversity and multicultural training has been implemented with the assertion that they are meant to reduce further injustices against this marginalized other. While such prerogatives may appear to be attempts to address acts of prejudice and discrimination, we would like to consider how these initiatives are potentially more insidious acts of marginalization because of their implicit adherence to the discourses of cognitive science. The subject in the era of social justice as premised by these discourses is the subject of conscious intention and bias to the exclusion of the unconscious. This is not surprising. The unconscious and the subject of the unconscious has seen little notoriety in 21st-century westernized countries. However, this exclusion of the unconscious as the seat of subjectivity actually constitutes the subject as in allegiance with neoliberal capitalist demands, which flattens difference and particularity in exchange for enjoyment as the foundational injunction on all subjects, and at the expense of the expatiation of historical complaints.

Diversity Training and the Starbucks Incident

Diversity and inclusion training has been a part of workplace policy and procedure in a variety of settings for some time. However, recently a news story went viral that launched such training into the headlines, allowing for public debate and speculation about what this type of training claims to do. On April 12, 2018, Donte Robinson and Rashon Nelson, two black men, were arrested at a Starbucks in Philadelphia after the manager called the cops on them. The young men said that they were there to meet their friend, but the manager said that because they had not purchased anything, they were trespassing. The incident was caught on tape and quickly went viral. The young men settled with the city of Philadelphia for $1 apiece and a promise to launch an entrepreneurship program (Donnelly, 2018). Shortly after, on May 29, Starbucks decided to close the doors of 8,000 of its franchises for one day in order for their employees to undergo diversity training. They also released their diversity training curriculum, continuing to suggest to the media that this was an attempt to address an issue both within and beyond Starbucks. This initial training was intended to be the first step in an ongoing commitment to issues of diversity and inclusivity. The training day, according to their website, employs the use of tool kits, drafted by experts, for employees to use in self-guided groups, followed by a film directed by Stanley Nelson depicting African American history and experience. Groups use a manual that guides conversation and an iPad which shows videos feature various personalities such as Starbucks CEO Kevin Johnson and rapper Common and tracks the groups' progress through the different tasks.

While the Starbucks approach may have been the most publicized, its approach to diversity resembles many of the ongoing workplace diversity training programs already established. While Starbucks may employ celebrities like Common to narrate their videos, and include more opportunities to reflect on what makes us all different, the point of the training is essentially to elaborate on implicit bias, though in this document it is problematically referred to as unconscious bias, with the intended promise of helping people "overcome their unconscious brain" (Starbucks, 2018, p. 22). The goal is also to emphasize and promote places in which the most number of people are included. Starbucks emphasized this with a graph in which employees are asked to consider who is not present in their store and what could be done to make them feel welcome. Similarly, the hope for workplaces is that a large number of people can co-operate in spite of their different races, genders, sexual proclivities, and so forth.

Concerns about diversity and inclusion are crucial. As articulated earlier in this book, discrimination and prejudice are problems built into the fabric of our social institutions, which needs to be adequately addressed. Furthermore, as psychologists, the concern with social justice and equality is intimately tied to our discipline. Even psychologists who are not therapists or overly involved with the clinical side of psychology would likely say that they have a general concern for the reduction of harm and suffering an individual goes through or is exposed to. Many psychologists have attempted to consider and address these issues either explicitly or implicitly in their curriculum or research. This is to say that, in many cases, the intentions of psychologists are likely to be good. However, the means through which those intentions are expressed may inadvertently cause more harm than good, especially when they do not consider human subjectivity in all of its contradictory and ambivalent responses to the aporia of lack.

Diversity initiatives, and approaches to bias reduction implicitly rely on principles articulated within cognitive psychology as a sort of common sense, obscuring the debates within the discipline of psychology itself, as well as mistaking theory for fact. Fundamental to these approaches is an assumption about how to correct for bias once it has been identified. The Starbucks manual mentions in two distinct occasions that the purpose is to rid bias from the unconscious brain. This approach assumes that a bias is something that has eluded conscious thought processes, which can be accounted for by providing a systematic set of rules that will help identify biases by checking one's own behaviors. These rules are then deployed in a variety of scenarios in which the person undergoing the training is expected to either imagine or watch a hypothetical situation in which a transgression has occurred. Furthermore, if these rules are not effective enough, there is the reassurance that the rest of the office staff is being trained to identify and report the offending behaviors, along with an evasive sliding scale of reprimands. When cognitivism fails, behaviorism is deployed.

Diversity training is not only relegated to the office workplace. Most states require counselors seeking licensure to have training in multicultural counseling. While issues of social inequalities and injustices are something everyone would ideally be exposed to, multicultural counseling seems to attempt to provide future counselors with a sampling of issues that would pertain to those groups identified as culturally diverse. A survey of textbooks dedicated to the topic of multicultural approaches to counseling illustrates that such courses and training are designed to first identify those groups belonging to the culturally diverse, surprisingly there are typically about 12 to 15, which seems to correspond nicely to the standard amount of chapters in a textbook. These chapters then provide an overview of those rituals and habits within those groups that a multicultural counselor or clinician should know in case they present in the therapy room. The assumption seems to be that such habits and rituals may read as symptomatic to a person who is not familiar with them and lessens the amount of time the client or patient may need to spend explaining aspects of his or her culture to the therapist. In both the cases of the diversity training and multicultural counseling, the assumption seems to be that issues of discrimination and prejudice can be accounted for through knowledge about those identified as an outgroup. This assumption will be taken up further in this chapter.

The Cognitivist Approach to the Other

It is this privileging of knowledge about the other that needs to be interrogated by those of us interested in social justice and psychology. In fact, this type of relationship to the other premised on knowledge encapsulates the heart of the problem of cognitive science and its inability to address issues of racism and sexism. The research coming out of cognitive science on racism, sexism, homophobia, and so forth revolves around theories such as implicit bias, social categorization, scapegoat theory, category-based perception, and other social cognition models which all posit a subject who, for whatever reason, needs to think differently. Allusions to the unconscious or unconscious biases, such as in the cases of implicit biases and scapegoat theory, conveniently disregard theorization about the subject of the unconscious. Instead, they favor the assumption that once one is tuned in to their biases and mental shortcuts that lead to decision-making errors, they will inevitably change their thoughts to change their actions. Techniques to address such problems include cognitive restructuring and neural rewiring (Boscardin, 2015; Bosman, 2012).

It may not be immediately obvious why such an approach that promises the reduction of workplace, or in the case of Starbucks, national discrimination is a problem. However, it is important to note that despite the overwhelming rate of adoption of such practices, there has not been a lot of promising results from diversity and sensitivity training as indicated by the fairly stagnant instances of prejudice and discrimination at the workplace (Dobbin & Kalev, 2018). This is an issue in and of itself, with a question of whether or not such initiatives may actually increase such occurrences. If we are to respond as the behaviorists assume, then pairing mandatory, usually dry and tedious tasks, along with threats of punishment, with a constant identifiable group or groups, it may stand to reason that those undergoing the training may learn to associate those groups with the affect produced as a result of said training. Furthermore, approaches premised in cognitive science approaches also construct the subject as a closed circuit of concepts, rules and glitches, and despite the trend in these approaches to use the word "unconscious" interchangeably with the word "implicit," there is little consideration for the actual subjectivity of this computer person, that is, the thing which actually throws the switch in the first place—the unconscious. As Dalal (2012) explains, cognitive behavioral approaches function as a sort of symptom reduction, failing to address or account for that which the symptom signifies. We would like to further suggest that what these sorts of approaches do is not simply reduce symptoms but instead demand an instantiation of a new symptom. Furthermore, the issue with such theories is, according to philosopher Slavoj Zizek (1989), is that people typically know what it is that they are doing and continue to do it anyway, regardless of whether or not the thoughts or behaviors are prejudicial or discriminatory. In contrast, psychoanalysis may allow us to consider why knowledge, for example about racial bias, fails to deter the individual from acting prejudicially and instead consider racial bias as a symptom manifested by a subject who does not know his or her investment in such a symptom in the first place.

Psychoanalytic Theory and Politics

This chapter attempts to consider the social and political ramifications of diversity and inclusion initiatives and discourses on those it attempts to assist from a Lacanian psychoanalytic perspective. Lacan was no stranger to social theorization and dedicated an entire seminar to consider the role of psychoanalysis in the social sphere. Many contemporary psychoanalysts and social theorists have also urgently advocated for a consideration of our political climate through Lacanian psychoanalysis, believing that it cannot only address pertinent issues but can also offer insight when certain projects aimed at alleviating the suffering of relevant groups may actually be contributing to said suffering. Hook (2017) argues that jouissance, a Lacanian term for the unconscious enjoyment that is simultaneously premised in pleasure and suffering, occurs within language and meaning making systems and is fundamentally concerned with the functioning of the Lacanian law/ paternal metaphor and the Superego. He argues that racism is demarcated by an overinvestment in the other's jouissance, or the pleasure and suffering derived from functions of their culture, perceived or otherwise. George (2016) identifies the jouissance of the other as a motivating factor in the shooting of Jordan Davis in Florida in 2012 by Michael Dunn. From prison, Dunn wrote numerous letters about the excessiveness of the rap music Davis and his friends were listening to in their car prior to Dunn opening fire. George suggests that assumptions about jouissance might allow for a consideration of racialized identities. Jouissance offers a means to think about the unconscious apprehensions of the other, that goes well beyond theories of implicit bias. The reason for this is because the jouissance of the other is only threatening because it reminds one of the ways he or she is existentially incomplete, or what Lacan referred to as lacking.

Along with the notion of jouissance, Lacanian psychoanalysis also offers a way to consider symptoms and pathology as not simply intrinsic to the nature of human subjectivity, but constituted between subjects and social discourses. Within the Lacanian clinic, one can be diagnosed as a neurotic, psychotic, or pervert. Within neuroses are the further distinctions hysteria and obsessional neurosis. For our purposes here, we will contain our explanations to neurosis, and more specifically to obsessional neurosis. In Lacanian psychoanalysis, the neurotic structure comes into existence through repression, specifically the thoughts that are attached to certain affects become repressed. Anxiety is the originary affect that fails to be repressed and is always in relation to repressed thoughts directed at or about the primary Other, who both grants you what you desire, as in the case of the infant crying to be fed, and enjoys you past the satisfaction of your desire, as in the case of the infant who is full but cannot remove himself or herself from the source of food. Anxiety can be said to be present when one is reminded of one's own lack or when confronted with the (O)ther's jouissance, (O)ther denoting that it may not be the original Other's enjoyment, but any other which prompts the subject to re-experience that stifling enjoyment by the Other. Once a thought is repressed, it becomes attached to other thoughts and experiences through an unconscious network of associations. The specific neurotic structure, hysteric or obsessional, arises out of the characteristic ways of attempting to manage this anxiety when faced with those associations with the repressed content. More specifically, the subject arises out of an encounter with the primary Other, and the ways that the subject comes to understand that relationship determines the subsequent structure. Symptoms, from this perspective, are not simply manifestations of illness but signifiers addressed to the Other, the unconscious placeholder for the primary caregiver to whom all early utterances were addressed. An appreciation for Lacan's understanding of pathology, therefore, offers a means through which to consider the manifestation of social discourses as attempts to address the Other.

Obsessionality

As mentioned, the discussion here is best limited to the obsessional structure because of its similarity to the cognitive science approach's attempts to deal with encounters with difference. The obsessional structure is constituted by a negation of the Other. As all neurotic structures are organized around a lost object, which for our purposes here can be understood as the thing that would make one whole but is irretrievable. According to Fink (1999), the obsessional refuses to acknowledge that the lost object is related to the primary Other and thus believes himself to be self-contained and mistakes himself as whole. Any reminder of his fundamental lack is deeply anxiety provoking. This occurs typically through an encounter of difference, that is, with one's own unconscious as evoked through an encounter with an other's unconscious. In order to manage this threat to his existence as he knows it, he is compelled to neutralize or destroy the Other, specifically the desire of the Other, that questions his assumptions and exposes his own lack (Fink, 1997). The question that the obsessive formulates in relation to the fundamental question "What am I?" is "Am I dead or alive?" as Fink (1999) explains, "the obsessive is convinced that he is, that he exists, only when he is consciously thinking" (p. 122).

The neurotic's symptoms are those disruptions and interruptions of speech and behavior that indicates there is repressed content to begin with. Obsessional symptoms can take on a variety of characteristics and as mentioned, typically involve some sort of unconscious and symbolic killing of the (O)ther. Fink (1999) explains that for the obsessive the original disturbing thoughts may not necessarily be entirely repressed, but rather the link between thought and affect are broken. This means that the return of the repressed is likely to return in the realm of thought for the obsessional, in contrast to psychosomatic symptoms for the hysteric, and that he denies his, and others', unconscious. To quote Fink (1999):

> The obsessive, as conscious thinker, deliberately ignores the unconscious— that foreign discourse within us, that discourse we do not and cannot control, which takes advantage of the ambiguities and multiple meanings of words in our mother tongue to make us say the opposite of what we consciously meant, and do the opposite of what we consciously meant to do.
>
> (p. 122)

Obsessional symptoms attempt to expropriate the presence of the Other in one's own unconscious and subjectivity. The obsessional believes that he is complete unto himself, and therefore tends to be preoccupied with masturbation, both sexually and intellectually. Because of this, obsessionals tend to fixate on stringent rules and the accumulation of knowledge, usually that which manages both his and others' desires. Desire, because it is derived from the original lost object which resides in the Other, is implicitly threatening to the obsessional. The quest for knowledge becomes an obsessional project when it attempts to account for both the one's own subjectivity and others'. For example, theories which emphasize the gendered mating rituals, habits, and preferences of human beings from an evolutionary psychology perspective could be regarded as obsessional because they attempt to neuter the enjoyment of the other. That is, they neutralize the desire of the object of study, in this case the human being in a sexual context, and the observer can presume to know the course of action, and most importantly, what is desired from him.

Diversity and inclusion training, as well as some attempts to account for multiculturalism in the therapy room, seem to reflect this desire to account for the other through knowledge and thereby proactively prevent the person or persons in the position of Other from having any sort of presence or effect in their own singularity. That is, individuals belonging to the groups "woman" or "minority" tend to be replaced with knowledge about those groups, and subsequently, interactions and reactions to those individuals belonging to said groups are governed by the rules generated by such knowledge. Inclusion, sensitivity, and empathy premised in knowledge about who or what the other is inevitably reifies categories of exclusion such as race, gender, and sexual orientation through its stultification of difference. Actual difference between and within subjects is drained from living bodies and instead abstracted into signifiers and commodities that allow us to interact with that which we believe we know—that is objects constituted by knowledge to the exclusion of a confrontation of desires. This is perhaps some of the subtle subversiveness of Black Lives Matter, to which "All Lives Matter" was a swift response. With Black Lives Matter, there is a radical specificity that the "All" cannot account for, because no "All" exists. In comparison, diversity initiatives premised on inclusivity could be said not to be celebrating diversity because their agenda is premised on an assimilation of all under neoliberal capitalism.

In assuming this is an obsessional endeavor, it can also be assumed that repression is still at work. As explicated earlier, though repression for the obsessional functions to separate thoughts from affect, it maintains its affect because the primary thought or thoughts associated with the repressed material have not yet been excavated. That is, the associations embedded within the connections to the original thoughts become the material for the obsessional to remark on consciously because they are not "it." In the case of diversity and inclusion projects, the original provocation that elicited behaviors directed at those in the position of Other is not represented in the training manuals and videos, but they deal instead with the schemas, concepts, and observable biases and in doing so take on the form of an obsessional neurosis.

However, such initiatives also reflect the cognitive science tradition's overwhelming persuasiveness on contemporary assumptions about subjectivity, which is particularly insidious for those of us concerned about social justice issues. Foundational to these approaches to racism, sexism, and other such prejudices is the assumption that the subject thinks before he speaks, rather than, as we see in psychoanalytic thought, thinks through his speech. Prejudicial attitudes and acts of discrimination are the result of a malfunction of the information processing system that guides thought and behavior. This concept of subjectivity posited by cognitive psychology adopts a Cartesian dualist perspective, in which the mind and body are split and in which, as Parker (2015) explains, "reason is viewed as operating from a single point of certainty best, as a condition for its own pre-eminence, by doubt" (p. 15).

Parker's work *Psychology After Lacan* highlights a number of issues that Lacanian thought exposes about cognitive approaches to subjectivity. Thought for Lacan is what is articulated through speaking, and thus language is not simply a medium through which to transmit ideas from one mind to another. An interpretation based on one's own subjectivity, and thus unconscious, always intercedes any one-to-one experience of language. Language, given to us by an Other, is always alien to us and therefore always produces a sense of lack from our inability to adequately convey ourselves to another. Parker states:

> The symbolic order is always "other" to us, and so a Lacanian conception of the unconscious is of it as the "discourse of the Other"; it is a relay of desire and site of individual cognitive "accomplishments" (to use an ethnomethodological term) as well as communicational activity. A shift to "practical cognition" (Lave, 1988) is not sufficient to account for the role of the symbolic order and its effect in the human subject as the domain of the unconscious.
>
> (p. 16)

This is why any vestige in the unconscious thought in relation to language, which notions such as "implicit bias" in cognitive approaches claim to do, is antithetical to most psychological explanations of cognition. As Parker goes on to demonstrate, this also means that the ego or the subject of conscious thought as opposed to language does not have a privileged perspective on the motivations of the subject. For Lacan (1988), the ego is a symptom, "the human symptom par excellence, the mental illness of man" (p. 16). The ego can be understood as a callus formed on the psyche, built up with defense mechanisms and symptoms formed by habit and familiarity that protects the unconscious, but which should not be mistaken for the subject, just as the callus formed on the hand from lifting weights should not be mistaken for the source of strength that lifts the weight in the first place. Attempting to ascertain one's own biases and attitudes, without considering the ways in which those attitudes and biases serve unconscious desires and drives, is the equivalent of picking a callus on one's own hand—it may become tender, but will in all likelihood grow back if one continues to lift weights.

Obsessionality, Cognitivism, and Neoliberal Capitalism

If the cognitive-obsessional approach to diversity and inclusion actually maintain rather that challenge the issues they claim to address, then what is their purpose? We do not want to suggest that such initiatives are actually conspiracies to maintain unequal power distributions among the sexes and races, even if they do reify such categories and thereby are inherently problematic. However, by demonstrating the obsessional neurosis latent within such projects, the problematic construction and relationship to those demarcated Other can be excavated. This, however, does not quite explain the overwhelming popularity among social institutions and corporations to include some sort of diversity and inclusivity training as part of the workplace initiation. The obvious answer is that it is good for business. Businesses that are proactive about prejudice and discrimination are seen as ethical and socially responsible. This is how diversity and inclusion becomes a neoliberal project, rather than a compassionate one, aimed not at harmony among disparate groups but seclusion in the name of productivity. The cognitive model of subjectivity lends itself easily to the neoliberal capitalist obsessional venture because from this perspective, subjectivity premised in a conscious and knowable object can be manipulated, dare even disciplined and punished in the Foucauldian sense, accordingly, to align with contemporary demands.

Diversity and inclusion studies originate in management studies, a discipline dedicated to ensuring that managers initiate best practices in order to glean the most amount of productivity out of their workers. The Conference Board of Canada (2019) understands diversity as "an essential business function to be accounted for within corporate strategy. Diversity and inclusion is a business driver as well as a promoter of well-being, customer satisfaction and innovation." This subtle nounification as indicated by the use of the word "is" as opposed to "are" exposes the insidious capitalist rhetoric. Diversity and inclusion are no longer nouns, indicating an action taken on the part of concerned individuals, but a commodity one possesses. This is perhaps most evident in the Starbucks example previously given, but it can be seen in a number of corporate environments—academia and the counseling room among them. As we discussed earlier, neoliberalism has created a culture in which students are expected to chase credentials. Diversity and inclusion is now one more credential that someone can possess, as opposed to a continuous collaborative exercise between oneself and others. This of course makes it more difficult to actually confront issues of systemic inequality and oppression because such businesses and workers will now have a piece of paper to exonerate them from any wrongdoing, just as the subject constructed by cognitive psychology can examine one's own thoughts to determine if their action was motivated by bias or not. As Freud tells us, however, rationalization and displacement are very convincing defense mechanisms.

Finally, research has demonstrated that rather than challenging dominantly held beliefs and practices against those they claim to assist, diversity policies and procedures end up reifying systems of exclusion premised on prejudicial discourses (Iverson, 2007). In research on educational policies advocating diversity, Iverson (2007) demonstrates the ways in which such policies tend to perpetuate problematic discourses about people of color. She argues that many diversity discourses tend to portray people of color as implicitly outside of the institution, at-risk victims, commodities, and "change agents." She goes on to demonstrate that institutions frequently engage in group comparisons, with the white majority being the standard against which people of color are measured. From a Lacanian perspective, such discourses are latent with the jouissance of enjoying the other's perceived lack, all the while attempting to negate one's own. In measuring success rates in people of color against those standards set by white achievements, and then constructing people of color in ways that emphasizes a lack, these discourses serve to keep those deemed as lacking as forever lacking. The issue, however, is that Lacan tells us that lack is all speaking beings' ontology. Discourses that are posited on a fundamental vulnerability of one group over another only serve to obfuscate the vulnerability over the supposedly privileged. I say supposedly here only to demarcate this ontological lack, and do not dispute that there is a very real material privilege held by dominant groups.

Creating out-groups as a way to promote productivity in the workplace are not new. As Parker (2007) states, "There has always been a close link between capitalism and racism, and the employment of 'aliens' in the new industries during the early development of capitalism also inspired employers to use divide-and-rule tactics to separate workers from each other" (p. 60). Separating workers, especially based on racial groups or sex and gender, ensures an out-group premised on difference that has been essentialized, rather than on a more obvious contentious relationship—that of the worker and the employer. Though advocating for an environment in which all are welcome is not inherently a problematic venture, when that environment is exploiting individuals for their labor, it may be cause to pause. One way to ensure that the exploitation of individuals is not the focus of public ire (e.g., as in the case of adjunct professors at universities and colleges) is to promote discourses of inclusion which assert that the company, workplace, and so forth is one of which all would want to belong to in the first place, further obscuring any contentions about whether the exploitation of labor for capital may be something activists want to have more people reject. Diversity and inclusion training allows for the systematic checking in with one's own thoughts and biases, which puts the impetus on the individual to account for systemic issues that reinforce neoliberal subjectivity. Foucault (2010) uses the term "governmentality" to discuss the ways in which governments and institutions use social control to reinforce hierarchical power distributions and ideologies. He suggests that neoliberal governmentality allows for greater social control because individuals no longer need oppressive state forces to govern them, but rather they govern themselves through self-surveillance. From this perspective, if workers are reminded of the ways in which they can violate the terms set forth by diversity and inclusion initiatives, and subsequently face the social stigma of being racist, sexist, or as we set forth in the next chapter, not "woke" enough, they are less likely to turn their attention to the inherently exploitative economic system behind the curtain, so to speak.

Is Empathy the Answer?

The question for psychologists who are both concerned about inequality and oppression in contemporary society, and are skeptical about the level of radical change cognitive science endeavors are actually capable of, is how to rethink social justice as an issue with subjectivity. We discussed earlier that cultivating compassionate, as opposed to sensitive, subjects may be one way to address such concerns. Sensitivity because it implies a certain awareness as a precursor to action, can be understood as a passive-aggressive response. If we understand that sensitivity seems to imply that one has knowledge of what the other's sensibilities are, and then reacts accordingly, sensitivity assumes a certain hostility or offense on the part of the other, allowing one to act before the other can give voice to his or concerns, if there be any. Compassion, in contrast (meaning to co-suffer), offers an opportunity to consider alterity in relation, to consider a subject constituted by lack, not from their own failures to succeed or find purpose, or any other notions we ascribe to a conception of "wholeness," but rather from an ontological inability to account entirely for an other, who is also unable to totally account for you.

In their work on empathy and ambivalence, Swales and Owen (2019) demonstrate that one of the great insights by Freud and other psychoanalysts is that the human subject is constituted by a great deal of ambivalence. They suggest that in foreclosing or denying that basic ambivalence in the name of injunctions to empathize, or to love thy neighbor, has symptomatic effects at both the individual and societal level. We hypothesize about what some of these symptoms may be more extensively in the following chapter, suggesting that degrees of "wokeness" may be one such example. Swales (2019) suggests that empathy functions as a master signifier, or a sign that contains meaning within itself and does not point to other signifiers in order for subjects to understand it or comprehend its value. In capitalist economies, the dollar sign serves as a master signifier. Empathy becomes packaged and sold as a product to address the distress experienced due to an ever-increasingly disconnected and isolated society. Swales tells us that it is a tool that can be acquired through purchasing the right books or attending the appropriate seminars, so that one can market themselves an "empath." Empathy, just as sensitivity and inclusivity, has become a tool to make you a more productive commodity. Empathy, and initiatives to cultivate it, will inevitably fail, Swales argues, if they fail to account for both one's own and the other's jouissance.

It seems that the spirit of social justice initiatives is heading in the right direction, with more people being concerned about the material and psychological conditions of those who have been systematically and systemically disenfranchised. However, we suggest that the means through which that spirit is actualized is inherently problematic because it fails to consider the subject as ontologically split. This can be seen in both our reiterations of Buddhist subjectivity, as well as the Lacanian theory of the subject. In what follows, we will take up the specific symptoms we see being manifested in contemporary Western society as a result of the failure to account for one's own ambivalence and contradictions through a Baudrillardian lens in order to further explore the ways in which subjects and society constitute one another.

References

Boscardin, C. K. (2015). Reducing implicit biases through curricular interventions. *Journal of General Internal Medicine, 30*(12), 1726–1728.

Bosman, M. (2012, August 8). Your racist brain: The neuroscience of conditioned racism. *Strategic Leadership Institute.* Retrieved from https://strategicleader. webnode.com/news/your-racist-brain-the-neuroscience-of-conditioned-racism/

Conference Board of Canada. (2019). *Diversity and inclusion.* Retrieved from www. conferenceboard.ca/topics/orgperform/research/diversity-inclusion.aspx

Dalal, F. (2012). *Thought paralysis: The virtues of discrimination.* London: Routledge.

Dobbin, F., & Kalev, A. (2018). Why diversity training doesn't work: The challenge for industry and academia. *Anthropology Now, 10*(2), 48–55.

Donnelly, G. (2018, May 24). Starbucks released part of it diversity training curriculum. *Fortune.* Retrieved from https://fortune.com/2018/05/24/starbucks-diversity-training/

Fink, B. (1997). *The Lacanian subject: Between language and jouissance.* Princeton, NJ: Princeton University Press.

Fink, B. (1999). *A clinical introduction to Lacanian psychoanalysis: Theory and technique.* New York, NY: Routledge.

Foucault, M. (2010). *The birth of biopolitics: Lectures at the Collège de France, 1978–1979*. London: Picador.

George, S. (2016). *Trauma and race: A Lacanian study on African American racial identity*. Waco, TX: Baylor University Press.

Hook, D. (2017). What is "enjoyment as a political factor?" *Political Psychology, 38*(4), 605–620.

Iverson, I. (2007). Camouflaging power and privilege: A critical race analysis of university discourse diversity policies. *Educational Administration Quarterly, 43*(5), 586–611.

Lacan, J. (1988). *The seminar: Book I: Freud's papers on techniques*. Cambridge: Cambridge University Press.

Lave, J. (1988). *Cognition in practice*. Cambridge: Cambridge University Press.

Parker, I. (2007). *Revolution in psychology: Alienation to emancipation*. London: Pluto Press.

Parker, I. (2015). *Psychology after Lacan: Connecting the clinic and research*. London: Routledge.

Starbucks. (2018). *Team guidebook*. Retrieved from https://hros.co/templates-upload/starbucks bias-training-workbook

Swales, S. (2019, October). *Empathy with extimacy*. Paper presented at Ecrits conference in Pittsburgh, Pennsylvania.

Swales, S., & Owens, C. (2019). *Psychoanalyzing ambivalence with Freud and Lacan: On and* off the couch. London: Routledge.

Zizek, S. (1989). *The sublime object of ideology*. New York, NY: Verso Books.

5 "I'm Just Not Woke Enough"

A few years ago an acquaintance of mine made a post on social media in which she spoke of some recent inner struggle and exhaustion with trying to stay on top of all the current ways in which her privilege blinded her to the oppression of an ever-growing number of groups. Moreover, she fretted over the myriad ways in which she might be slighting those groups, particularly unintentionally, and at the end causing her to exclaim that she was just not woke enough. Such a situation is by no means unique to this individual; it has even been the topic of a satirical comedy sketch by famed British comedian Tracey Ullman, which portrays a "support group" for people who are so "woke" that they can no longer function or relate to others. Phenomenon such as these have led me to believe that social justice is no longer a facet of a left/liberal ideology, but it has become an ideology unto itself and with a problematic kind of subjectivity.

As was mentioned in the introduction of this book, the idea of social justice has been around for quite some time, but it found particular purchase during the 18th and 19th centuries with the arrival of a new ways of thinking about one's subjective place in the world, particularly the advent of the women's emancipation movement, class/economic equality, and the abolition of slavery (Walsh, Teo, & Baydala, 2014). However during those times, and even during its 20th-century iterations, these movements have been part of larger ideological systems (e.g., Liberalism and Socialism/Marxism). During the 21st century there appears to have been a shift in which social justice has become an ideology unto itself, a point that shall be elucidated shortly.

It might be helpful here to define what is meant by ideology, as it has many connotations and almost as many definitions as it does commentators. In common parlance, ideology is simply the ideas that undergird a system of thought. These undergirding foundational ideas are typically taken as universal givens from which social, economic, and governmental/political systems are then structured. For the purposes of my argument I am borrowing heavily from Lacanian philosopher Slavoj Zizek, who designates it as

> anything from a contemplative attitude that misrecognizes its dependence on social reality to an action-orientated set of beliefs, from the indispensable medium through which individuals live out their relations to a social structure to false ideas which legitimate a dominant political power.
>
> (Zizek, 2012, p. 3)

What Zizek is getting at here is that ideology need not be dependent on reality itself; as long as the subscribers to that ideology take it to be true, it is enough for them to orient their lives and organizational structure around it. To put it another way, Zizek in *The Sublime Object of Ideology* says, "The function of ideology is not to offer us a point of escape from our reality but to offer us the social reality itself as an escape." To illustrate this with an example, one need only look to the social movement of social Darwinism. Social Darwinism is the idea put forward by British philosopher Herbert Spencer, the man who coined the now famous term "survival of the fittest," who utilized Darwin's theory as a way of explaining societies' current trends and difficulties, both past and present. At its base, social Darwinism is supposed to be founded on the principles of the evolution of species through natural selection, wherein, to put it simply, variation within a species leads some organisms to have better access to resources, increases their likelihood of survivability, and thus they are more likely to reproduce and pass on those variations to offspring. Social Darwinism takes these founding principles that apply to biology and nature and makes a philosophical, not empirical, equivalency to human societies, as if a society is analogous to an organism in nature. Thus a society, armed with this pseudoscientific understanding of Darwin's well-documented biological principles of adaptation and survival, could now be justified in doing everything in its power to reproduce itself, fight and kill for limited resources, including the destruction, enslavement, displacement, and oppression of "lesser" societies and cultures, seeing them as weaker or less fit "organisms" (see Walsh et al., 2014, pp. 188–190). Darwin himself opposed such thinking in his own writings (cf. Darwin, *Voyage of the Beagle*, chapter 21). We can now see how ideology is at play, the social realties that social Darwinism created, and were and are largely accepted and utilized by most of Western societies, allowed for a social reality that did not require an escape from necessary confrontation with the atrocious reality of slavery, genocide, and culture erasure; rather it made it the status quo. Implicit in this notion of ideology is that it is not just societies as a whole that fall prey to this (mis)recognition of reality but also the individual at the subjective level. The idea that subjectivity, how one defines one's self in the world, is also influenced and molded by ideology is the among the central tenets of the post-Enlightenment philosophers such as Marx, Nietzsche, and some time later, Freud. Marx in particular would critique the capitalist ideology and mark the foundational ideas for a new kind of subject as one who thinks socially, not individualistically, and lays what will become part of the groundwork for the modern social justice movement.

However, today's social justice is now facing a number of problems that were not faced by its 19th- and 20th-century predecessors. This is in part because, like the social justice movements of the 19th and mid-20th centuries, they share the same motor of one of Marx's primary critiques: if injustices hidden by ideology could be exposed for what they are, and the facts of reality to the world sufficiently demonstrated, then people would awaken and would engage in revolutionary change. Such was the power behind women's suffrage movements and later the civil rights movements, in which they assumed the utopic meta-narrative: the truth of the "end of history." However, along with this narrative a new wrinkle appeared at the end of the 20th century, founded in the works of philosophers and critics such as Lyotard, Foucault, Derrida, and others. The critiques of modernist thought that these thinkers provide established a mode of thinking which will come to be known as postmodernism. These new discourses are still with us today in the 21st century. Walsh et al. (2014) contend that this new approach came about as a direct opposition to the ideas of modernism's three dominant thought systems of positivism, utilitarianism, and dialectical materialism: "[Comte's] Positivism, with its virtual worship of natural science; [John Stewart Mill's] Utilitarianism, which quantified happiness to create the greatest good for the greatest number of people; and [Marx's] dialectical materialism, with its biblical day of judgment, the socialist revolution" (p. 163). In contrast to these three, postmodernism offers up the critique of these notions with the idea that there is no grounded "truth"; the new motor powering social reality is, as Jean-François Lyotard put it, an "incredulity towards metanarratives."

A full exposition on variations of the ideas/philosophies that lie under the umbrella of postmodernism is beyond the scope of this text, however in *The Passion of the Western Mind* (1991), Richard Tarnas provides an easily digestible summary, quoting Ihab Hassan. Tarnas writes:

> [Postmodernism is] an antinomian movement that assumes a vast unmaking in the Western mind . . . deconstruction, decentering, disappearance, dissemination, demystification, discontinuity, difference,

dispersion, etc. Such terms . . . express an epistemological obsession with fragments or fractures and a corresponding ideological commitment to minorities in politic, sex, and language. To think well, to feel well, to act well, to read well, according to the episteme of unmaking, it to refuse the tyranny of wholes; totalization in any human endeavor is potentially totalitarian.

(p. 401)

This approach, Tarnas (1991) goes on to explain, opens up a wide pluralism in which new ideas are allowed to grow, "provid[ing] less hindrance to the free play of intellectual creativity." However, he goes on to state that "fragmentation and incoherence are not without their own inhibiting consequences. The culture suffers both psychologically and pragmatically from the philosophical anomie that pervades it" (p. 409). One such harbinger of the dangers of this position was Jean Baudrillard.

In his seminal work *Simulacra and Simulation*, Baudrillard puts forward an idea that dovetails neatly with our working concept of ideology, that of hyper-reality. Baudrillard argues that current culture is quickly heading toward, if not already in, a place where the simulation of reality replaces real reality altogether, and there is no way to tell the difference. This is similar to the aforementioned misrecognition of social reality, with the crucial difference being that there was never an attempt to ground it in a reality, to give it a referent (e.g., the biological principles of natural selection that ground social Darwinism). Rather, it is a fantasy, imaginative art, which is then misrecognized as true real, a false reality indistinguishable from the reality with no means of telling them apart. To paraphrase philosopher Marcus Pound (2018), Baudrillard's notions of a false reality, a simulacrum, "is seen in the way culture and media rather than imitating life, are now flipped and life imitates media." Given that Baudrillard's work predates social media, one could easily add that this applies to social media such as Facebook as well, if not doubly so. This postmodern reality is without a metaphysics, but it is also a reality immune to critique, as there was never a reality to which one can point as a referent to judge it against. This notion of a non-critiquable reality has become a new driving force for subjectivity and one that directly affects our examination of social justice.

Just as modernism laid the groundwork for the individualistic and rational subject, by establishing a social reality loosely based in the natural science, the various threads of postmodernism opened up the door to critique, or rather deconstructed, the notion of self, identity, and even subjectivity—and herein lies the problem for 21st-century social justice. On one hand, its heritage comes with a heavy reliance on Marxist thought and assumptions, for its ideas surround a social, and not individualistic, idea of subjectivity. This is evidenced in the rise of socialist leaning political candidates who, along with their supporters, are highly vocal proponents of social justice movements and initiatives, and admirably fight for the rights, recognition, and visibility of oppressed minority groups by trying to show how these groups are suffering under systemic problems—like systemic racism and sexism—an argument not that dissimilar to Marx's argument of the proletariat under the bourgeoisie.

On the other hand, the postmodern critique, with its ever-deconstructing processes at play, has caused a cacophony of new voices who each claim oppression and demand distinguishment and recognition from within these very minority groups. However, given the impossibility of establishing a base from which to evaluate these claims, as the postmodern distrust of meta-narrative is wont to do, social justice becomes self-stultifying. We see this exemplified in the ever-growing list of identities in identity politics, in what Lacanian terms we might call the ever-slipping signifier of oppression; each marginalized group dividing and subdividing. There are two warring ontologies, two foundational assumptions, which stand diametrically opposed in the social justice movement of this new moment in history.

But can we claim that social justice has in fact taken up the status of an ideology in its own right? Has it misrecognized the functioning social reality for the reality it is trying to operate in? And what about the hidden division within the movement's very philosophical framework—does this proffer any clues to the question? Perhaps; the idea of such a warring division within one system is not new one; in fact, it is the basis of Freud's theory of psychodynamic thought.

If one were to look at the movement as if it were a subject of the analysis, the subject of social justice is divided upon itself, both desiring and repressing those desires at the same time, then this conflict would be announced by the arrival of a symptom. If we then apply psychoanalytic theory to the social order, as Freud did in *Civilization and Its Discontents*, then we should see cultural symptoms arise from this movement. And in fact two such symptoms can be pointed out with relative ease.

Since all are not necessarily versed in psychoanalytic thought, it might be helpful to outline what is meant by symptom. In a technical sense, in a person a symptom can be thought of as a piece of unspoken desire that returns from the unconscious. To put it simply, if we take up Lacan's idea that the unconscious is structured like a language, then the symptom could be thought of as being structured like a metaphor—a message from the Subject that is delivered to the Other (God, the Universe, etc.) while they are seemingly addressing some other person with whom they are interacting. This might be something like a declaratory or performative act or statement, which seems out of place or off-kilter. Much like when an actor in a play breaks the fourth wall and speaks to the audience, but the other characters on stage, who also witness the actor speaking and acting, don't understand to whom the actor is actually talking, and in this case neither does the actor himself, as it is an unconscious address. One is left asking, "why are you telling me this or doing this?" Or in more modern lingo, "that's a weird flex, but OK."

When looking at this from a larger viewpoint such as the symptoms of an ideology, Zizek (2008) puts it this way: "The symptom is, strictly speaking, a particular element which subverts its own universal foundation, a species subverting its own genus" (p. 21). As stated previously, the symptom is going to be unconscious and it is not recognized by the subject. This is epitomized in what has been called Starbucks consumerism, that is, maintaining a consumerist attitude, buying overly priced coffee in disposable cups, while being able to show the world in a highly visible way, vis-à-vis that recognizable cup, that you "care" because you drink coffee that is fair trade and the cup is recyclable. Similar to this flex is the "Facebook activist" who puts a filter on their profile picture or a rant about injustice as their status and then calls it a day, feeling they have done their part.

This latter example in fact is the first of the symptoms pertaining to the social justice movement. It goes by many names: the Tumblr Social Justice Warrior, the Facebook Activist, the call-out troll, and so forth, wherein social justice causes are seen as an opportunity for social performance rather than a chance for participating in actual activism.

Symptom 1

These individuals demonstrate their subversive nature, as a species working against its genus, in that they actively work against one of the primary tenets of social justice: the desire for equality of inclusion. Such individuals make use of internet forums and social media to "call out" oppression or bias when they see it. However, this is not done in the spirit of education or to help someone become aware of a heretofore unseen privilege, rather it is used as a bullying tactic and a chance to try and belittle and ostracize individuals. All this is done while operating under the protective umbrella of "fighting for the cause" and being a member of a marginalized group. Such a strategy is sometimes referred to as punching up. Whether such practices are right or wrong is beyond the scope of this paper, but they are certainly displaying themselves as symptoms.

To illustrate, in 2014 a controversial exposé written by Laura Mixon rocked the science fiction and fantasy writer community. A well-known anonymous social justice "rage blogger" who had caused recognized and award-winning authors to fear putting pen to paper, was found to be an author named Benjanun Sriduangkaew, a prominent member of their community. To quote one report, "She frequently resorted to graphic threats of murder, rape, mutilation, acid attacks, and other extreme violence. . . . [One author] was branded a 'rape apologist' whose 'hands should be cut off so she can never write another Asian character'" (Young, 2018).

In one online community, dedicated to books by people of color, when Sriduangkaew

> viciously insulted an author or a fellow community member, she framed it as bravely speaking out against racism and other injustices. . . . If she could not immediately find anything in a person's comments to twist and misconstrue, she would simply accuse them of being white. If they responded that they were not white, she would accuse them of being mixed race or no longer living in the country of their ancestors. Only she was an authentic person of color, and only she could judge what was racist and what was not.
>
> (ibid.)

It is abundantly clear that such behavior is unreasonable, but it was in the reaction of the moderators of this community that we see the problem of a social justice system founded on the tenets of postmodernism, in which critique is impossible. To further quote the report, the site's moderators

> worried that by telling [our troll] she couldn't do this stuff anymore, they would be silencing a person of color who had a right to be angry about injustice. They eventually put up an "Insults Policy" post explaining that you couldn't insult community members for no reason, but that it was OK to "snarkily" call them out for being racist, sexist, etc.
>
> (Young, citing Mixon (2014))

The worry of the moderators was not unfounded and was a laudable effort in reflection, one that attempts to avoid the false consciousness that Marx succinctly describes in *Capital* in his quote, "They do not know it, but they are doing it." They did not wish to perpetuate the status quo of oppression, and yet we see the conflicted interplay of the Marxist assumptions with the deconstructionist approach wherein even the Marxist notion—that the oppressed need to band together to enact the revolution, not attack one another—could be interpreted as one more oppressive power tool founded in principles of white privilege.

The report further outlined that a number of these cyberbullying episodes significantly targeted more "women, people of color, and other marginalized or vulnerable people" more than cis white men (Mixon, 2014). Although this report was contested by a number of online bloggers who argue that Sriduangkaew's statements have been misunderstood, misrepresented, and the result of white supremacy trying to stifle a person of color's voice in the guise of fighting for "true" social justice, the interesting part is, as is always the case in hyper-reality, the empirical truth is actually irrelevant. No matter which side is the side of "truth" or real representations of social justice, neither can actually make an appeal to reality; as Baudrillard argued, even that would be a mere simulacrum and not reality itself. We can see what Zizek was getting at here, as a species that subverts its own genus. Because of actions like those of Sriduangkaew's and others like her who use the principles "social justice" as a method for "call-out trolling" and often have a louder voice then, say, those of active social justice scholars and political activists, the (mis)recognition of what social justice is by the general population and the new media, who may view such actions as threatening or a tool to maliciously politically manipulate others, causes the movement to trip over itself.

Symptom 2

In turning our attention to the second symptom, we can step back from the problematics of critique in a postmodern zeitgeist and turn more squarely to the problem of dealing with the competing assumptions at the heart of 21st-century social justice, which is the exhausting nature of forever performing the tasks of being "woke," or never being woke enough. As mentioned in the opening story, there is an interesting phenomenon in the ideology of social justice in which one feels compelled to be "woke," or aware of every possible infraction for every possible minority or less represented group. A noble task to be sure, but in fact an impossible one given how quickly new "identities" are created, and even knowing the impossibility of the task it does not stop individuals from making the attempt. In this we see another argument that social justice has reached the status as ideology, for as Zizek said, riffing off of Marx, "they know it, but they are doing it anyway." In other words, these "woke" individuals proceed toward the task of "waking" themselves and others in a traditional Marxist fashion as if to uncover reality underneath. Nevertheless, they also know that after this elephantine process of waking and seeing how privilege and power has blinded them to the suffering of whichever minority or oppressed group they are examining, they will only find that the pachyderms go all the way down. So the question is why? How is it that this new social reality compels its subscribers to continue at the work in perpetuity? To answer that one might turn again to psychoanalysis and the power behind the mandate of the Superego.

Freud introduced the concept of the Superego in 1923 with the publication of *The Ego and the Id*, wherein he lays out his structural model of consciousness. In this work Freud contends that the Superego is an unconscious agency that forms after the child concedes to the ultimatum that she/he cannot be what fulfills their mother's desire, and must recognize law, or in other words social prohibitions. This enables the child to "transform her/his cathexis of her/his parents into an identification with them—she/he internalizes the prohibition" (Laplanche & Pontalis, 1974, p. 436). To enforce these prohibitions placed upon the subject by society, the Superego wields guilt as an unconscious weapon.

However, in contrast to Freud's early 20th-century version of the Superego, an agent of prohibition, which was rooted in Enlightenment-era thinking, Lacan's ideas of the mid- to late 20th century reexamines the subject's superego, now being influenced by a new zeitgeist, and finds an agent of command, particularly the command that you must enjoy. Now to be clear, enjoyment here is not mere pleasure, such as enjoying a fine meal, rather it is what Lacan labeled as jouissance, the pleasure that must be experienced to the point of excess, which you enjoy against your best interest. Evans (2006) elucidates the difference, saying:

> The pleasure principle functions as a limit to enjoyment; it is a law which commands the subject to "enjoy as little as possible." At the same time, the subject constantly attempts to transgress the prohibitions imposed on his enjoyment, to go "beyond the pleasure principle." However, the result of transgressing the pleasure principle is not more pleasure, but pain, since there is only a certain amount of pleasure that the subject can bear. Beyond this limit, pleasure becomes pain, and this "painful pleasure" is what Lacan calls jouissance; "jouissance is suffering." The term jouissance thus nicely expresses the paradoxical satisfaction that the subject derives from his symptom, or, to put it another way, the suffering that he derives from his own satisfaction.
>
> (p. 93)

Or, as my nine-year-old son put it after overeating his favorite food to the point of stomachache: "My pizza has too much jouissance."

Zizek speaks of it as the reversal of the Kantian imperative changing: "We all know the formula of Kant's unconditional imperative: "*Du kannst, denn du sollst.*" You can do your duty, because you must do it. Superego turns this around into "You must, because you can.""

So how does this translate to the ad infinitum cycles of getting "woke" experienced by the ideological subject of social justice? Why do they engage in an ever-growing list of self-imposed thought and language policing that is often seen within the movement? Zizek (1999) contends this is tied directly the notion of the Superego:

> The concept of the superego designates precisely this mysterious overlapping in which the command to enjoy overlaps with the duty to enjoy yourself. Maybe we can in this way distinguish the totalitarian from the liberal-permissive superego. In both cases, the message is "You may enjoy, but because you may, you must." In both cases you pay a price for this permission. In permissive liberalism, the "you may" of freely inventing yourself is paid for when you get caught in the cobweb of prohibitions concerning the well-being of yourself and your neighbors. We can do whatever we want today, hedonism and so on, but the result is that we have at the daily level so many prohibitions so as not to prevent others from enjoying. *You are constantly told what to eat and drink, no fat, no smoking, safe sex, prohibition to enjoy the other, prohibition of sexual harassment, and so on, life is totally regulated. . . .* It's the postmodern subject of total permissiveness who gets caught up in so many prohibitions that precisely in order to be happy.

Thus in age of absolute moral freedom in which as Nietzsche says, "God is dead," or in this case metaphysics are gone, then as Dostoyevsky says *The Brothers Karamazov*, "Without God . . . everything is permitted." However, Lacan's reversal is what has actually been realized "If there is no God, then everything is prohibited."

When we apply this idea to the postmodern half of the modern social justice assumption engine, we start to see the nature of the symptom of "ever-waking" and its necessity in order for the whole ideological construct to maintain its cohesion. The self-imposed secular morality of thought and language policing stands in as a flimsy ground from which social justice's ideologies can reflect on and still offer "critique" of those who do not participate in and use the latest politically correct vocabulary and modes of thinking. But in order to do this, it must be constantly engaged with the ever-shifting categories of the aggrieved and, unconsciously, enjoying the ever-growing list of their grievances. To paraphrase Slovenian philosopher Alenka Zupancic, one is not just drowning in opportunities to be woke, because there are so many and it is difficult to choose between them, it is precisely because we are to somehow not miss out on any chances to demonstrate we are woke. Thus we can argue that being "woke" has entailed in it a huge amount of enjoyment, and like the first symptom is a species that goes after its own genus, it is an enjoyment founded in the exclusion of others, directly contrary to the ideal position of social justice.

To illustrate further, Alenka Zupancic (2016) has spoken about the fantasy of the last cigarette, a fantasy of ending, in that the idea that it is the last, therefore it is better than any other.

Is this not similar in enjoying ones generation, as the last in which African-Americans . . . gay African-Americans . . . trans-gay African-Americans . . . etc. are discriminated against? The generation that is on *the right side of history*. This notion of *the last* demonstrates that it is enjoyment itself that is what is being enjoyed. One might imagine the Subject of social justice saying to themselves, "this will be the last time/ chance I have to be woke, therefore I can revel in my wokeness one more time." And as the hallmark of any symptom is its need for repetition, this of course creates an endless need for more wokeness, in order to maintain enjoyment. Thus a new category of minority or victim needs to be found in order to maintain this structure of enjoyment. One more thing with which to police one's thoughts, one more word to excise from one's vocabulary, or one more inclusive neologism to add to it. To again paraphrase Zupancic (2016). "You want to stop you really want to stop, but you end up accumulating one more after another, thus you end up infinitely repeating the end, and enjoying it against your will." This, she continues, is the very economy of the unconscious, the very notion of Lacan's drive: "the end is inherent of the repetition and the repetition is inherent of the end."

The question then becomes not just the obsession with ending the injustice, but rather the obsession with being part of the culture surrounding the ending of social injustice. This leads to the classic double bind of the Subject who wants to have its cake and eat it too. The possibility of reaching a point of an end of obligation to the oppressed thus creates a never-ending parade of oppression categories, because of the superegoic demand to enjoy. In other words, the problem could be stated as: because there is the possibility of end it makes it never-ending. So what does one do?

The presence of these cultural symptoms seems to confirm that social justice has in fact reached ideological status and has some very real problems. These problems have arisen because of its conflicting assumptions rooted in both early 20th-century Marxist and 21st-century postmodern thought.

It has become adept at finding grievances but few solutions. This symptom of creating a parade of grievances, which are loaded with a kind of enjoyment, has caused the movement to struggle with making any real change, or as one 20th-century theologian put it, "Letting off steam always produces more heat than light" (Maxwell, 1989). The next question is whether or not the ideals of social justice are salvageable, such as the humane and fair treatment of all individuals.

The answer to this question may be that we must paradoxically abandon our quest for equality and embrace inequality. It may be to turn ourselves toward an infinite obligation, such an obligation to help the Other that would serve to quell the needs of the social injustices suffered by the oppressed. However, unlike the Marxist notion, dare I say fantasy, like that of the last cigarette, that one day such needs would be fully satisfied; this infinite obligation to help the Other never ceases. This not in the endless repetitions of superegoic enjoyment, which unconsciously relishes in suffering, but one in which one seeks to always prevent the suffering of the Other. Such an idea and system of ethics can in fact be found in the ideas of Emmanuel Levinas,[1] particularly in his notion of the face-to-face encounter with the Other.

The face in Levinas's thought is not a mere encounter with another person in a particular context. Rather, it is pure signification, a "signification without context." Levinas (1985) summed it up best in *Ethics and Infinity*, saying,

> Ordinarily one is a "character": a professor at the Sorbonne, a Supreme Court justice, son [or daughter] of so, and so, everything that is in ones passport, the manner of dressing, of presenting oneself. And all signification in the usual sense of the term is relative to such a context: The meaning of something is in its relation to another thing.

(p. 86)

Is this not the epitome of what we have come to understand identity in our social justice age? Are we not constantly reducing ourselves as this identity, or that identity, or in Levinasian language, totalizing ourselves, to the comparison of others? Identity is used like a crutch to ground ourselves into any kind of personal meaning in an era when our misinterpretation of social reality has stripped our subjectivity, reducing it to being only a creature of commanded enjoyment; a creature that must enjoy according the "character" roles of the context we find ourselves in. But Levinas offers a basis for subjectivity that is in fact much grander in scope. "The face," says Levinas, is meaning all by itself. You are you. In this sense one can say that the face is not "seen." It is what cannot become content, which your thought would embrace; it is uncontainable, it leads you beyond. It is in this that signification of the face makes its escape from being, as a correlate of knowing.

(ibid., p. 86–87)

Thou shalt not kill ME, the face implores. It is this encounter with the face that creates subjectivity itself, a demand for responsibility that exists before ontology, what Levinas called meontology, an "ethical peculiarity [that] is a rupture of being" or an ethics that exists beyond the bounds of being itself. To describe this rupture's effect on us, Levinas (1985) says:

It is an order. There is a commandment in the appearance of the face [Thou shalt not kill], as if a master spoke to me. However at the same time, the face of the Other is destitute; it is the poor for whom I can do all and to whom I owe all. And me, whoever I may be, bat as a "first person" I am he who finds the resources to respond to the call.

(p. 89)

In this new ethics, there is an infinite obligation to the Other that does not and cannot be sloughed off or ever truly finished, as we owe to the Other everything.

This is contrary to the usual way of constructing an ethics in a programmatic way, à la Husserl, following rules in which the ontology, in the Heideggerian sense, is neutral, which then gives rise to epistemology and then to axiology or ethics. In other words, we first establish what it means to be, then to know what is true, and finally to what is worthy; or in this case, what is worthy behavior. For Levinas this notion of ethics was part and parcel for what he called the philosophies of totality. That ethics/responsibility could be summed up to this or that correct behavior or to use this or that correct terminology in your discourse. Even when taking into account the postmodern notion of non-definitive truth, Levinas (1985) tells us that even this is an attempt at totalizing the subject: "Even if the truth is considered as never definitive, there is a promise of a more complete and adequate truth" (p. 91). The notion of the many "my truths" is in itself a meta-narrative that the idea many truths is the Truth. The hidden assumption of current social justice ideology is that it seeks in the end to neutralize all difference. As if in prophecy, Levinas's remarks apply to the plight of the social media acquaintance who can never be woke enough: "Without doubt, the finite being that we are cannot in the final account complete the task of knowledge"; in this case to know, account for, and correctly address all oppressed groups. He continues: "but in the limit where this task is accomplished, it consists in making the other become the Same" (p. 91). In it we see again how symptoms of ideology eat their own, when diversity is supposed to be prized by social justice, in reality what it seeks in the end not more diverse but rather all the same. But it need not be so.

Levinas's ethics that precede ontology can change this predicament. "Ethics does not supplement a preceding existential base; the very node of the subjective is knotted in ethics understood as responsibility" (p. 95). This encounter with the face and its obligation, an encounter that brings us out of solipsism and into being, can halt the symptom of the ad infinitum division of oppression and collections of marginalization (who is gayer, blacker, more oppressed, or in the case of the trolling, you are not gay enough, not black enough, not woman enough). Each face demands an infinite obligation. This gives a freedom from finding the end of obligation to the oppressed, changing the demand of the Superego to the demand of the Other.

However, in this change it cannot be seen in something as simple as changing "Black Lives Matter" into "All Lives Matter," in which the eponymous "All" is faceless, it changes to "This Life Matters," "This" referencing the current face in view, and no matter how much you do for that individual it will never absolve of your responsibility to do ever more. Rather, to further quote Levinas, "It is I who support the Other and am responsible for them . . . my responsibility is untransferable, no one could replace me. . . . Responsibility is what is incumbent on me exclusively, and what humanly, I cannot refuse."

By postulating an ethics-first approach as Levinas does, we arrive at a different notion of subjectivity, and a more Hegelian notion of ideology, in which one can never truly escape ideology. As there is always something in ideology that is self-defeating, there is always something additional, something excessive, that you can never really account for. Just as in the Sriduangkaew case in the science fiction/fantasy community in which any attempts to equalize the playing field, to punch up against oppression, results in creating the totalitarian subject, the dictator, who wants equality as they would dictate it to all. Thus a social justice system becomes a system for thought policing: all opinions are welcome except the ones that we don't like. Highlighting further the symptom that bedevils social justice as it argues for equal representation (democratic) it does not, in fact, want true equality; some voices it simply does not want to be heard and as was exemplified, it eventually turns on its own in an effort to further its desire.

Perhaps a Hegelian position might offer some insight into a solution. Most people are familiar with the Hegelian triad: thesis, antithesis, and synthesis. In a popular way of explaining Hegel's notion of dialectic method, two competing positions are shown in play (thesis and antithesis), and then a compromise is struck by blending aspects of the two (synthesis)—a kind of middle ground. The problem is, Hegel himself never used this triad, and this is in fact almost the opposite of what Hegel had in mind. Rather, Hegel contends that we must come to terms with the fact that there is always a break, that there is never any way out of the polarization. To take a Zizekian turn and put a Lacanian spin on this, true synthesis is about coming to terms with lack. The trap that needs to be avoided, however, is to think that we are to come to terms with the fault in the other, in the minority, that the oppressed are simply to accept their lot in life. The argument here is not about accepting that you cannot change the oppressed's lot in life or in the systems of society; rather the opposite it is true. In the encounter with the Face of the Other, we will do all we can to improve their plight. Rather, it is precisely one's own lacking subject that one must come to terms with. That each person is always chasing desire, in this case equality, and never achieving it, but enjoying the ever-growing number of populations that need to be equalized, in the case of the "ever-waking" or the enjoyment of call-out culture and being able to lord over others lack of "wokeness." Both are responses to the lack in one's own subjectivity. In other words, in order for a social justice to function it must stop trying to be about equality, and it must end its repetition compulsion to try and "educate" others, and even perhaps oneself.

In regards to education, this holdover of Marxism, is in many respects like treating the symptoms of society that social justice seeks to address the way Freud spoke of physicians who attempted "wild" psychoanalysis. This happened, Freud said, when physicians who, only having a partial grasp of the psychoanalytic process and its theories, tried to cure their patients' neurosis by telling them about psychoanalytic theory, and to quote Freud, "these measures have just as much influence on the symptoms of nervous complaints as the distribution of menus has on hunger during a famine" (Freud, 1920, p. 205). Education practiced in social justice ideologies does not provide a cure to the symptom; at worst it is ineffective, and at best it simply moves it. The "woke" may no longer enjoy certain things, for example, words that are considered micro-aggressions, but as has been already pointed out, they will continue to enjoy the oppressed as a source for finding new things to be woke to, and they need them to always be oppressed to continue their enjoyment. We must awaken[2] to the Face of the Other, to their demand for care. However this must include all by all, even the neo-Nazi, the racist, sexist, and the unwoke, for as Levinas would have us understand, one cannot sum up the totality of their being into categories such as these, for to do so is only to perpetuate the symptom.

It is such a Levinasian position that I contend is the way in which we as a society could perhaps find our way out of problematic notions embroiled in the subjectivity of our current social justice ideology and escape the symptoms of dueling philosophical assumptions. To close, I will end with the quote which closes Levinas's chapter on responsibility for the other in *Ethics and Infinity* from Dostoyevsky: "We are all responsible for all men before all, and I more than all others."

Notes

1. A full discussion of Levinas, his philosophy, and his ethics is simply beyond the scope of this work. It is not my intent here to be exhaustive, rather to be accessible. For this reason I have chosen to use *Ethics and Infinity* as the main text, as it is arguably the most accessible introduction to his philosophy.
2. Levinas frequently used the metaphor of sleeping, waking, and insomnia to describe subjectivity. However only the Other could wake us from solipsism and into subjectivity—another reason one is eternally indebted to the Other.

References

Evans, D. (2006). *An introductory dictionary of Lacanian psychoanalysis.* Abingdon: Routledge.

Freud, S. (1920). *Selected papers on hysteria and other psychoneuroses* (A. A. Brill, Trans., 3rd ed.). Lancaster, PA: The New Era Printing Company.

Laplanche, J., & Pontalis, J. B. (1974). *The language of psycho-analysis.* New York, NY: Norton.

Levinas, E. (1985). *Ethics and infinity: Conversations with Philippe Nemo* (R. A. Cohen, Trans.). Pittsburgh, PA: Duquesne University Press.

Maxwell, N. A. (1989, October). *Murmur not.* General Conference of the Church of Jesus Christ of Latter-day Saints, Salt Lake City. Retrieved from www.churchof jesuschrist.org/study/general-conference/1989/10/murmur-not?lang=eng

Mixon, L. J. (2019, April 24). *A report on damage done by one individual under several names.* Retrieved November 11, 2019, from http://laurajmixon.com/2014/11/a-report-on-damage-done-by-one-individual-under-several-names/

Pound, M. (2018, May 8). *Postmodern philosophy and theology* [Video file]. Retrieved from https://youtu.be/qTzOsi8bQCw

Tarnas, R. (1991). *The passion of the Western mind.* London: Pimlico.

Walsh, R.T.G., Teo, T., & Baydala, A. (2014). *A critical history and philosophy of psychology: Diversity of context, thought, and practice.* Cambridge: Cambridge University Press.

Young, C. (2018, August 18). The forgotten story of how "punching up" harmed the science-fiction/fantasy world. *Quillette*. Retrieved from https://quillette. com/2018/08/18/the-forgotten-story-of-how-punching-up-harmed-the-science-fiction-fantasy-world/

Zizek, S. (1999, August). *The superego and the act*. Lecture transcript. Retrieved from https://zizek.livejournal.com/1101.html

Zizek, S. (2008). *The sublime object of ideology*. London: Verso.

Zizek, S. (Ed.). (2012). *Mapping ideology*. London: Verso.

Zupancic, A. (2016). The end. *Provocationbooks.com*, (1), 1–9. Retrieved from www.provocationsbooks.com/2016/10/31/the-end/

Index

consumer services 50
corruption 9
critical psychology: on contemporary
culture 28; counter-narrative of 7–9;
goals of 44; on individual-focused
psychotherapy 35; insights from 49;
on social reform 29; subjectivities
and 4, 44; on systemic apathy 20
culture: anxiety and 28; capitalism
and 28, 31–32; community-focused
healing and 7; consumerism and
28; critical psychology on 28;
democratic 7; individualism and
28; narcissism in 28; neoliberal
7; postmodernism and 68;
psychological theory or practices and
10, 12; social character and 12–13;
subjectivities and 11–14, 19–21;
transformative paradigm framework
for examining 21–22
Cushman, Philip 5, 28, 29, 31, 33, 35,
37, 44
cyberbullying 70–72

Darley, John M. 16–18, 20
Darwin, Charles 66
Davis, Jordan 54
Deikman, Arthur 40
democratic culture 7
depression 12, 28, 31
deregulation 7
Derrida, Jacques 67
dialectical materialism 67
discrimination 52–53
displacement 59
diversity 1, 13, 16, 59, 77
diversity initiatives 5, 13, 50–60
divide-and-rule tactics 60
doctor–patient relationship 7
domination 7, 12
Dostoyevsky, Fyodor 74, 80
dualism, Cartesian 57
Dunn, Michael 54

ecopsychology 35, 44
education: competitiveness in
4, 11; contemporary models
of 13; diversity in 1, 13, 59;
diversity initiatives in 13; false

consciousness in 17–19; injustice
gap and 16; IQ tests in 15; market
rules for 7, 16; neoliberalism and
8, 11, 59; pluralistic ignorance
in 18–19; power hierarchies in
10; privatization of 16; in social
justice ideologies 80; standardized
testing in 12, 15–16; subjectivities
construction in 11; systemic apathy
in 14–16, 18–19; tracking systems
in 19; vouchers for private school
tuition 16
Ego 4; *see also* Superego
ego: divine lack and 37; injustice
and 34; Lacan on, as symptom 58;
quieting 40, 44; self and 33, 39;
subjects and 58; unconscious and 58;
see also superego
Ego and the Id, The (Freud) 73
egotism 34
empathy 9, 30–31, 40, 57, 61
emptiness 5, 28, 31–33, 36–42
empty self: advertising and 33;
alternative approaches to
37–38; neoliberalism on 49;
psychotherapeutic treatment of 28,
33, 37, 44; as a social construction
38–39; subjectivities and 5, 39
epistemology 77
equality 70, 76, 78–80
equality movements 65
equity 16
equity initiatives 13
ethics 33–34, 76–78
Ethics and Infinity (Levinas) 76, 80,
80n1
ethics of care model 30
ethnicity 16
evolutionary psychology 56
exclusion 57, 60
exploitation 12

Facebook 68
Facebook Activist 5, 70
false consciousness 17–19, 71
false generosity 21, 22
Fink, Bruce 55–56
Foucault, Michel 11, 14, 31, 60, 67
fragmentation 37